THE CHATEAUX
OF THE LOIRE

66 locations - 321 photos

PRODUCTION
LECONTE

VALOIRE publications
PRINTED BY LECONTE
BLOIS 41260 LA CHAUSSEE-ST-VICTOR

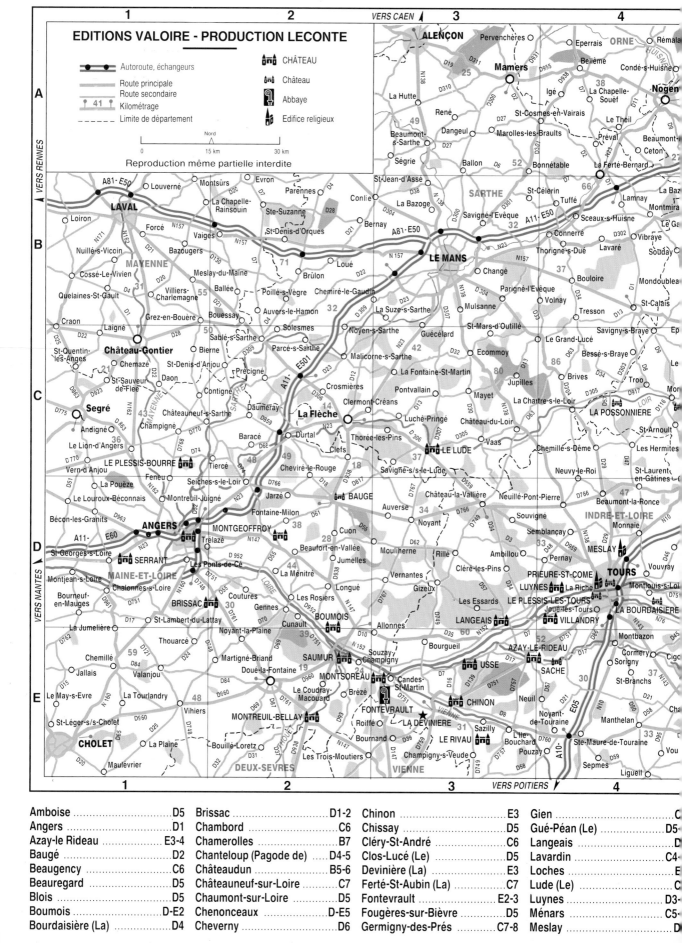

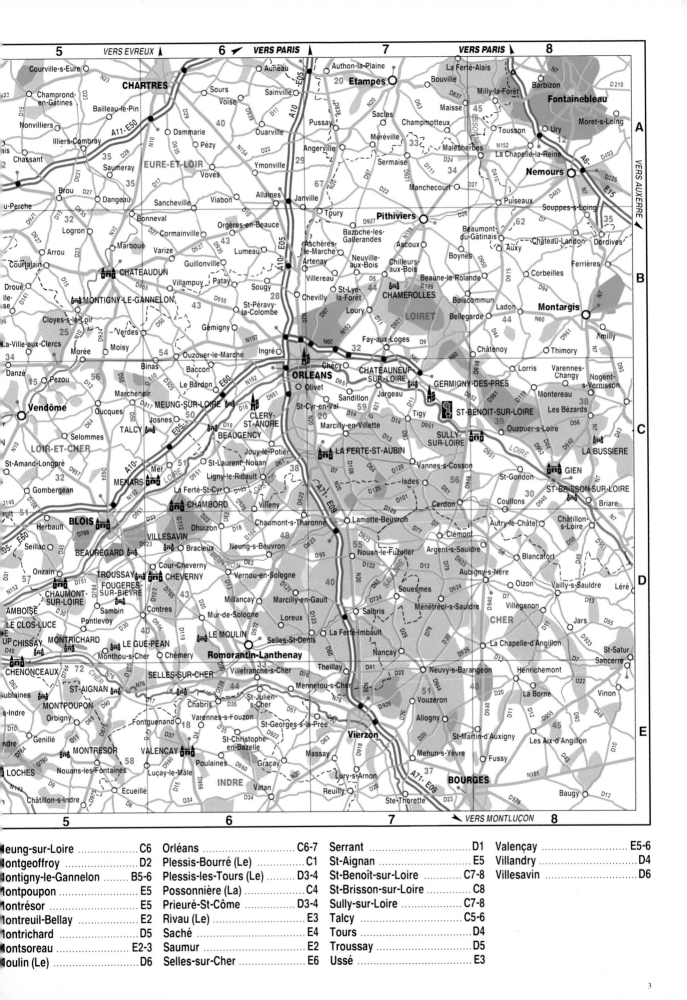

THE LOIRE

The area of the castles of the Loire valley extends over three ancient provinces: Orléanais, Touraine and Anjou, and down as far as the north of Berry.

It is outlined around the great loop which the Loire forms, moving up towards the northwest, from Gien to Orléans, then down to Anjou. Its tributaries, the Loir, the Cisse, the Cosson and the Beuvron, the Cher, Indre and Indrois, Vienne, Thouet, Layon and Maine complete the main section of the river and define a vast, rich area, united by its history.

After the Gallo-Roman peace, the barbaric age commenced, followed by restoration of power by the Merovingians, and finally the Carolingian Renaissance. During these centuries of upheavals, the valley of the Loire was an important seat of development and of the spread of Christianity, with the start of the apostolate of Saint Martin, bishop of Tours, who died at Candes in 397. The setting-up of a church, which inherited the Roman civilisation, administration and language, was accompanied by the introduction of a clerical hierarchy and power, naturally spiritual, but also capable of replacing faultering earthly power, of gathering together the population, of tackling invaders, and finally of supporting the restoration of a lay order, providing the Merovingian, and later Carolingian princes with most of their ministers. This role of the clergy is testifed by the Roman and pre-Roman abbeys, priories and churches which line the river and its tributaries. Throughout the course of history, bishops and abbots continued to counterbalance the power of the great feudal lords who, from the tenth to the twelfth centuries, contested Orléanais, Touraine and Anjou, the counts of Blois against the counts of Anjou. There are traces everywhere of their struggles, finally ended by Philip Augustus by annexing the heritage of Anjou. Alas this heritage led to the Hundred Years' War. The count of Anjou, Henry II Plantagenet, had received the crown of England from his mother. His descendant, Edward II of England, having married Isabelle of France, daughter of Philip the Fair, last of the Capetians, his son in turn claimed the crown of France, worn by the Valois cousins.

During this eventful war, the Loire valley (Orléanais, Berry, Touraine and Anjou) was the trusted refuge of the French side: Paris, the capital of the kingdom, had surrendered to the Anglo-Burgundians, mad King Charles VI was their hostage. Charles VII, the dauphin, moved his fragile power and the royal administration to the Loire, travelling endlessly, as was the custom of the monarchy up to the eighteenth century, from one town, one castle, to the other, so that from Gien to Chinon, Saumur or Angers, the King felt at home. Thus, from one end of the Loire area to another, we come across him. Princes of royal blood, great lords, ministers and servants, under his reign or that of his successors, bought and built, creating an exceptional wealth of historical castles.

From the Loire Valley (where he was based) Louis XI rebuilt, stone after stone, his kingdom and re-established centralised power. His son, Charles VIII, opened the Loire valley to the influence of the Italian Renaissance, discovered during campaigns in Italy. After him, Louis XII,

VALLEY

then Francis I and his successors, prolonged the union between the civilisations of France and Italy. Henry II married the Florentine Catherine de Médicis. The calamities of the civil war, with a religious pretext, bloodied the valley in the second half of the sixteenth century, but did not jeopardise the prodigious expansion of the region which, even after the return of power to the Ile de France, which had begun under the reign of Francis I, kept its privileges of a Royal seat.

It is true to say that the castles of the Loire valley would not be the same without the sky, the landscape and setting: forests well-stocked with game for the royal hunts, providing wood for joiners, cabinetmakers and wheelwrights, pastures for the flocks, limestone plateaus providing quarriers and stonecutters with material for abbeys, churches, ramparts and castles. The ploughman found there deep land for growing corn in one place, and sandy ground for asparagus in another; orchards and vineyards enrich the well-exposed hillsides: from Gien to Angers virtually all the villages and castles will shower you with their local wine.

This landscape, shaped by more than fifty generations of peasants, is often threatened more than the monuments it surrounds. People are leaving the country, although an observant visitor can still meet descendants of those of our ancestors who can be seen ploughing, cutting, harvesting vineyards or killing pigs, sculpted on the Romans capitals, the tympana of cathedrals, the stalls of Gothic abbeys, the illuminations and tapestries of the fifteenth century. Talking to them, before it is too late and the last one has started to talk like the television, he will recognise the fine language of old France, so rich that it can be drunk in like wine and will remind him of the fruity prose of Rabelais or the nervous one, with its taste of gunflint, of the lampoonist Paul-Louis Courrier, the Tourange wine grower of Véretz.

Then, crossing the Loire, or travelling along it on the high stone embankments, we have to imagine it as it was up to the middle of the nineteenth century, endlessly carrying all sorts of fleets of boats down towards Nantes with the current, tacking close to the wind, with their huge rectangular sails billowing in the smallest breeze. There were the large sailing barges, measuring 30 metres by 5, carrying up to 60 tonnes, pine rafts which took down the freight never to return, sold for their wood, the flat-bottomed barges, turned up at both ends, and the barges for passengers.

The boats have disappeared after having seen the steamers travel along the river, paying homage, at Blois, to the memory of Denis Papin. The railway and later the roads have eliminated river trade and the highly individual boatmen of the Loire. The quays remain, with the heavy iron rings where their boats were moored, their houses in the suburbs, the lower part of the town, near the water. We have to imagine all these boats on the Loire as, on the roads, the carriages of merchants, the troops of soldiers, the caravan of the king moving to another castle, so long that the last carriage and the rearguard often passed by hours after the head of the convoy.

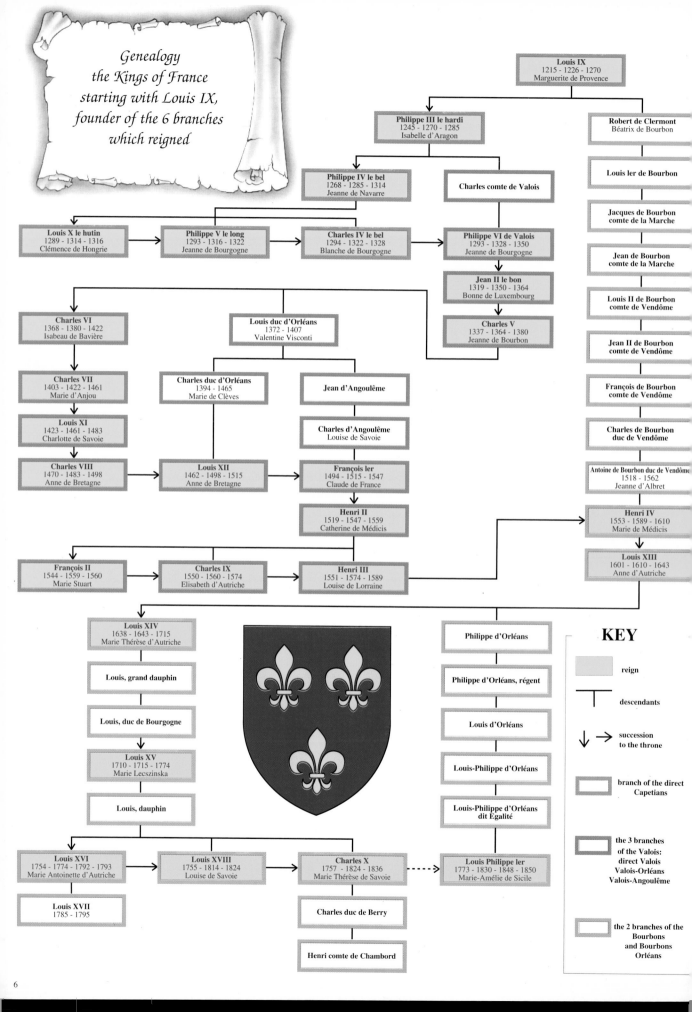

Genealogy
the Kings of France
starting with Louis IX,
founder of the 6 branches
which reigned

Louis IX
1215 - 1226 - 1270
Marguerite de Provence

Philippe III le hardi
1245 - 1270 - 1285
Isabelle d'Aragon

Robert de Clermont
Béatrix de Bourbon

Philippe IV le bel
1268 - 1285 - 1314
Jeanne de Navarre

Charles comte de Valois

Louis ler de Bourbon

Jacques de Bourbon
comte de la Marche

Louis X le hutin
1289 - 1314 - 1316
Clémence de Hongrie

Philippe V le long
1293 - 1316 - 1322
Jeanne de Bourgogne

Charles IV le bel
1294 - 1322 - 1328
Blanche de Bourgogne

Philippe VI de Valois
1293 - 1328 - 1350
Jeanne de Bourgogne

Jean de Bourbon
comte de la Marche

Jean II le bon
1319 - 1350 - 1364
Bonne de Luxembourg

Louis II de Bourbon
comte de Vendôme

Charles VI
1368 - 1380 - 1422
Isabeau de Bavière

Louis duc d'Orléans
1372 - 1407
Valentine Visconti

Charles V
1337 - 1364 - 1380
Jeanne de Bourbon

Jean II de Bourbon
comte de Vendôme

Charles VII
1403 - 1422 - 1461
Marie d'Anjou

Charles duc d'Orléans
1394 - 1465
Marie de Clèves

Jean d'Angoulême

François de Bourbon
comte de Vendôme

Louis XI
1423 - 1461 - 1483
Charlotte de Savoie

Charles d'Angoulême
Louise de Savoie

Charles de Bourbon
duc de Vendôme

Charles VIII
1470 - 1483 - 1498
Anne de Bretagne

Louis XII
1462 - 1498 - 1515
Anne de Bretagne

François ler
1494 - 1515 - 1547
Claude de France

Antoine de Bourbon duc de Vendôme
1518 - 1562
Jeanne d'Albret

Henri II
1519 - 1547 - 1559
Catherine de Médicis

Henri IV
1553 - 1589 - 1610
Marie de Médicis

François II
1544 - 1559 - 1560
Marie Stuart

Charles IX
1550 - 1560 - 1574
Elisabeth d'Autriche

Henri III
1551 - 1574 - 1589
Louise de Lorraine

Louis XIII
1601 - 1610 - 1643
Anne d'Autriche

Louis XIV
1638 - 1643 - 1715
Marie Thérèse d'Autriche

Philippe d'Orléans

Louis, grand dauphin

Philippe d'Orléans, régent

Louis, duc de Bourgogne

Louis d'Orléans

Louis XV
1710 - 1715 - 1774
Marie Lecszinska

Louis-Philippe d'Orléans

Louis, dauphin

Louis-Philippe d'Orléans
dit Egalité

Louis XVI
1754 - 1774 - 1792 - 1793
Marie Antoinette d'Autriche

Louis XVIII
1755 - 1814 - 1824
Louise de Savoie

Charles X
1757 - 1824 - 1836
Marie Thérèse de Savoie

Louis Philippe ler
1773 - 1830 - 1848 - 1850
Marie-Amélie de Sicile

Louis XVII
1785 - 1795

Charles duc de Berry

Henri comte de Chambord

KEY

reign

descendants

succession
to the throne

branch of the direct
Capetians

the 3 branches
of the Valois:
direct Valois
Valois-Orléans
Valois-Angoulême

the 2 branches of the
Bourbons
and Bourbons
Orléans

Portraits of the 13 kings descended from Charles de Valois, grandson of Louis IX and brother of Philip the Fair who succeeded to the throne of France, from the gallery of famous personages in the castle of Beauregard, near Blois.

Philippe VI de Valois

Jean II le bon

Charles V

Charles VI

Charles VII

Louis XI

Charles VIII

Louis XII

François Ier

Henri II

François II

Charles IX

Henri III

7

GIEN

GIEN, whose name recalls the important earthenware factory, founded in 1820, stands out with its characteristic outline on the right bank of the river Loire: the humpback bridge, built in the sixteenth century, the quays and the town, rebuilt after the bombing of 1940, and, above the brown-tiled rooves, the castle and the old church tower. A square tower at the southwestern corner of the castle recalls the feudal fortress which dominated the river, a strategic and trade route. The treaty of Gien was signed there in 1410 against the Duke of Burgundy, Jean sans Peur ("fearless John"), whom had ordered the assassination of Duke Louis of Orléans, brother of Charles VI, on 23 November 1407, in rue Vieille du Temple. Charles d'Orléans, son of the victim, formed an alliance, with his uncle, the Duke of Berry, with the Duke of Bourbon, his cousin, and the Duke of Brittany. Joan of Arc stopped there, on her way from Vaucouleurs, on 1 March 1429 and, at the end of June, with Charles VII, whom she led to Reims for the coronation. Francis I, leaving for Italy, stopped there to sign the letters conferring regency to his mother in his absence.

Louis XI gave the earldom of Gien to his daughter, Anne de Beaujeu, regent of France from 1483 to 1491, during the childhood of Charles VIII. She renovated the castle, from 1494 to 1500, apparently influenced by that of Plessis-Lès-Tours, built by Louis XI. Two main buildings of two storeys form a courtyard whose façades are punctuated by three polygonal stair turrets. The interior décor consists of multiple variations composed in their turn by red and black bricks and the white stones of the anchorages, at a time when stonemasons were normally content with using diamond-shapes of black bricks on red bricks, like in the castles of Moulin (15th C.), Blois (16th C.), or even chequers of stone and bricks, more common in Touraine.

The castle houses a hunting museum, with its exceptional collection of weapons and objects, and documentation on hunting, falconry and shooting. Desportes (1661-1743), painter of the hunting expeditions of Louis XIV, is represented by a group of admirable paintings and sketches. The museum also exhibits two paintings by his successor Oudry (1686-1755), one of which is the famous "Wolf Hunt".

A fine introduction to the discovery of the domains of the Loire valley, of the forests of Orléans, of Sologne, Touraine and Anjou, which rang out and still ring out at times with the sounds of the hunting horns and the baying of the packs of hounds, leaving in the morning from Chambord, Cheverny, Chaumont, Montpoupon, Brissac ....

▲ *Above: Museum of Hunting: "The Wolf Hunt" by Oudry.*
Part of the collection of trophies - "Hettier de Boislambert".

Opposite: earthenware vase decorated with palms. ▶

◀ *Left-hand page: the castle seen from the left bank - seen from the north east.*
The bronze stag from the foundry workshops of Seine-et-Marne (Museum of Hunting).

The barons of Sully paid their respects to the Bishop of Orléans and kept, on the left bank of the Loire, at the confluence with the Sange, a powerful keep, mentioned in historical documents, at the beginning of the 12th century. They controlled the bridge taxing travellers and merchants both on the road and on the river, so much so that the seigneury was confiscated by Philip Augustus, following complaints by ransomed merchants. The King commissioned a garrison tower to be built to ensure respect of his authority.

In 1382 the fief then came into the family of Guy de la Trémoïlle, who summoned to Sully, for advice, one of the architects of Kings Charles V and Charles VI, then commissioned the work from the family's master mason, who built the keep, courtyard and bailey, most parts of which can still be seen today.

His son, George, scheming favourite of Charles VII, often received the King there, who was at Sully when Joan of Arc liberated Orléans on 8 May 1429. The Maid stayed there, more or less detained by la Trémoïlle, jealous of her influence, at the end of the winter of 1429-1430, and slipped away with a small loyal band to go and fight the Burgundians in Ile de France. It was then that she was captured, at Compiègne. In 1481 Louis XI was received at the castle by Louis de la Trémoïlle, Louis XII and Francis I were received by his son.

In 1602 Maximilien de Béthune, very powerful minister and friend of Henry IV, bought the land of Sully, which the King, four years later, raised to a duchy. He restored the castle, having suffered the wars of religion, adapted it to the times, modernising its defences, particularly by building on the town side the bailey known as the Béthune tower, against artillery fire. Sully, in order to write the "Oeconomies royales", a work dedicated to the reign of Henry IV, and publish it immediately, installed in the tower adjoining his study a master printer from Auxerre who worked under his supervision. Sully was the last great lord of France, who had the right to mint money.

Under the Regency, four generations later, the Duke of Sully, who had nothing of the austerity of his protestant ancestor, received here a highly libertine society in which the young author Arouet, later known as Voltaire, shone. This Duke demolished the tower of Philip Augustus, altered the building to the right of the entrance and filled in the keep moat on the courtyard side.

The castle was spared by the Revolution: the Duke, grandson of the previous one, flaunted progressive ideas and had demolished the lordly attributes to the castle, such as battlements and machicolations.

The Regional Council of Loiret, owners since 1962, ensure restoration, conservation and activities at the castle.

Four corner towers flank the rectangular keep of the castle, surmounted by a covered way on machicolations and with a pointed gable roof. It looks out onto the Loire to the north and the fortified courtyard of the small castle to the south. Its moats of running water still surround it on three sides, the moat at the courtyard having been filled in during the eighteenth century. Rebuilt in the sixteenth century, the small castle rests on the Sange tower, which forms the southeast corner of the building, and on a porch tower in the centre of the wing. A recent building links the moat, replacing an 18th-century building, burnt in 1918. A gallery leads from the Sange tower to the Béthune tower.

The extensive terreplein, surrounded by moats, previously formed the bailey and sheltered the group of outbuildings, the tower of Philip Augustus, and a collegiate church, rebuilt by Sully in the town. It was turned into gardens in the eighteenth century and leads to a fixed bridge, formerly a drawbridge, at the entrance to the small castle.

◀ *The Sange tower, the small castle and the east towers of the keep.*

Figures on the tomb of Maximilien de Béthune, Duke of Sully and of Rachel de Cochefilet, his wife.

▲ *Large upper room on first floor of keep.*

Dining room of small castle. ▼

The interior of the castle holds some interesting surprises, starting with the keep, containing overlapping rooms measuring 300 and 100 square metres, with impressive fireplaces. On the ground floor there are 6 tapestries - rare items from Paris workshops - which, among other subjects, portray the story of the beautiful Psyche with whom Cupid himself fell in love. This legend was also narrated by La Fontaine in the same period. The reception and feudal court room on the first floor was furnished and decorated for Maximilian of Béthune, first Duke of Sully. His ancestors are portrayed in *trompe l'œil* paintings in the embrasures, and the castle of Rosny where he was born decorates the chimney breast.

An iron door concealed behind panelling leads to the room from which the guards manoeuvred the portcullis, drawbridge and machicolations; it became the Duke's treasury in the 17th century, and has been a private chapel since 1934, when the mortal remains of the Duke and his second wife were brought there from Nogent le Rotrou where their tombs, reproduced here, were desecrated during the Revolution.

Also on the first floor is the 100 square metre King's Room, with Louis XIII furnishings and 17th century tapestries; its 17th century bed recalls a visit by the future Louis XIV during the Fronde. The self-same room was used by his grandfather Henri IV, who honoured the Duke of Sully with his friendship.

A staircase leads from the state rooms to the parapet, the realm of the sentries, where the wind whistles over a vast landscape. This is also the storey containing the timber roof frame, a 600 year-old masterpiece. The small castle, dating from a few years later than the keep, is reached through the 18th century wing, which was damaged by fire in 1918. The Duke of Sully had his bedroom here on the first floor, in a smaller, cosier setting. The decorations on the coffered ceiling show that the Duke was Grand Master of the Artillery and devoted to his King.

Some of the castle furnishings were put up for sale in 1942; they were bought by the Département, and have

The roof framework of the keep.

now been restored to their original setting. The mulberry bush theme used to decorate the dining room reminds the visitor that Sully, financier and master of the artillery, was also a leading economist who wished to promote agriculture and industry, symbolised by the silkworm tree. We cannot leave the parish of Sully without giving a thought to Maurice, born of a humble family, who became a priest, then Bishop of Paris under the name of Maurice de Sully in the 13th century, and ordered the building of Notre-Dame.

LA-FERTÉ-SAINT-AUBIN

The seigneury of Ferté Nabert (Firmitatem Naberti), fortress of Nabert, is documented around 989. In the sixteenth century La Ferté belonged to the d'Estampes family who, in 1575, handed over to a cousin, François de St-Nectaire, the land and the small castle built in the middle of the century. La Ferté name becomes Ferté-Seneterre, according to the pronunciation of that time.

Henri, son of François, commissioned, at the side of the small castle, a new and large building which remained unfinished by his death in 1662. Henri, his son, having become famous in all the battles and field-marshal in 1651, retired to his land raised to the status of duchy in 1665. Without finishing the castle built by his father, he constructed the two wings of the outbuildings opposite the entrance to the courtyard.

▲ The large drawing-room.

▼ The kitchens.

After his death in 1703, without an immediate heir, the estate was sold in 1746, to the Marshal de Lowendal, who found the castle in ruins. He moved into it after his victorious campaign in Holland and restored it during the remaining 9 years of his life, a neighbour of the Marshal de Saxe, to whom Louis XV had given Chambord.

His heirs sold it to the shipowner from Nantes, Nicolas Bertrand. Having become rich through the slave trade, he had bought a title of Gentleman of the King's Great Hunt and the estate of Ferté-Lowendal suited his rank.

His nephew, marquis of Coué, inherited it then emigrated during the Revolution. On his return, he found his property as he had left it, thanks to his manservant who had made a pact with the revolutionary committee of Orléans: appointed guardian of the seized goods, he had prevented anyone from touching it. The land then belonged to the Countess of Talleyrand Périgord who sold it to Masséna, son of the Marshal of the Empire.

The castle suffered various fates until its repurchase, in a pitiful state, by Jacques Guyot in 1987, who then devoted his time to renovating it and to restoring its touristic and cultural value.

ORLEANS

Orléans is a symbolic town, the first town of the kingdom after Paris, at one time united with the Crown, at other times the prerogative of the younger brother of the King and of his descendants, as was the case under Charles VI and up to the arrival of Louis XII, then under Louis XIII and Louis XIV until the reign of Louis-Philippe. It was above all the key town in the successful outcome of the Hundred Years' War, the one which freed Joan of Arc, the Maid of Orléans. There are only a few remains of the towers and walls of the fortress coveted by the English, but history is omnipresent: churches, convents, mansions and ancient residences, even the names of the squares and streets are evocative of the rich past of the capital town of Orléanais.

In the Loire valley, like in other regions, during the dark years from the third to the fifth century, which saw the fall of the Roman Empire and spread of the great invasions, bishops and monasteries had maintained a certain degree of administrative, social and economic coherence, preserving the ancient civilisation which was to embrace the new princes, kings and chiefs of the Frankish tribes. In this way the bishop of Orléans, Saint Aignan, warded off in 451 the hordes of Attila who besieged the town and Clovis, taking this same town in 498, extended the Frankish kingdom over the region by relying on the church whose faith he had adopted. The Orléanais region, with that of Ile de France, from then onwards formed the heart of the future kingdom.

NOTRE DAME DE CLERY

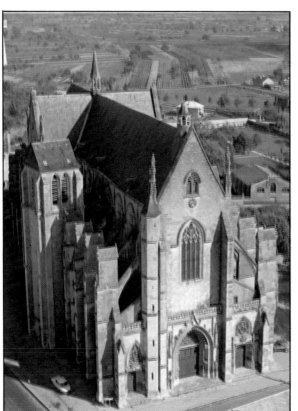

In one of the most turbulent periods of the history of France, when most of the Ile de France, cradle of the Capetians, including Paris, went over to the side of the Anglo-Burgundians, Orléanais, Vendomois and Berry remained faithful. For this loyalty Charles VII and Louis XI paid hommage to God, Our Lady and the saints. The basilica Notre-Dame de Cléry is proof of this, rebuilt in the fifteenth century on the site of a Marian pilgrimage church destroyed by Salisbury when he conquered Orléans. A few days later his head was blown off by a cannonball. The patrons of the reconstruction were Charles VII and the Count of Dunois first, and later and above all Louis XI, who wanted to be buried there with Queen Charlotte of Savoy. The whole church, completed by Charles VIII, was built in the fifteenth century, except for the square tower which the English did not succeed in destroying. It stands with great simplicity, luminous and pure. In the nave is the cenotaph of Louis XI at prayer, the work of Bourdin of Orléans and commissioned by Louis XIII to replace the original effigy destroyed by the Huguenots. The relics of the King are to be found in the neighbouring crypt.

SAINT-BENOÎT-SUR-LOIRE

The Abbey of Fleury, founded by Léodebod in 651 on a sacred site formerly venerated by the Celts, benefitted in 672 from the transfer of the relics of Saint Benedict from Monte Cassino to the monastery of the Loire valley. Abbot Théodulphe, bishop of Orléans, a close relation of Charlemagne, created the Benedictine schools there, famous in the West. The abbey was twice pillaged and burnt by the Normans in the second half of the ninth century. The construction of the present church of the abbey began with the porch tower which Abbot Gauzlin, son of Hugues Capet, built from 1004 to 1030, as a sign standing over the valley. The chancel was built under Abbot Guillaume in 1067; the sanctuary, chancel and transept were consecrated in 1108 and in the same year King Philip I, great-grandson of Hugues Capet, was buried in the chancel, where his recumbent statue can be seen. The whole church was consecrated under Abbot Barthélémy on 26 October 1218. The abbey, sacked by the English in 1358, 1363 and 1369 received Joan of Arc and the dauphin leaving from Sully for Reims in 1429. When the Revolution broke out, the buildings were sold and destroyed but the church remained with the parish. It was not until 1944 that a new Benedictine community moved there and rebuilt the monastery.

GERMIGNY-DES-PRES

The same Théodulphe abbot of Fleury, in order to escape on occasions the noise of the schools which he had founded, built, one league away from the abbey, his villa in Germigny and a small chapel, formed by four domed apses, under a lantern tower, whose openings illuminate the building, through sheets of alabaster. The Greek-cross plan and the construction are of Armenian Byzantine influence. The villa and small chapel, destroyed by the Normans, are in ruins apart from the east apse. In the fifteenth century a nave was added to the small chapel which had been rebuilt to be used as a church. The east dome was raced and the mosaic, virtually intact, hidden and thus protected, was discovered and restored in the nineteenth century, the only Byzantine mosaic of the ninth century in France. 130,000 cubes of light blue, gold, silver, purple and green compose the Arch of the Alliance which was guarded by two cherubs and two archangels with the hand of God stretching over them.

Above left: capital of the porch tower - St. Michael fights for a soul with Satan.
Right: the abbey-church of St-Benoît, seen from the southeast.

Below: the east apse of Germigny, interior and exterior.

MEUNG-SUR-LOIRE - The 13th-century castle, residence of the bishops of Orléans until the eighteenth century, was transformed, for the last prelates' pleasure, by the construction of large classical pavilions, supported by round towers, forming the main courtyard in the southwest. The apartments are furnished and decorated with paintings and tapestries. The vault of the guard rooms dates from the thirteenth century, as do the cellars, dungeons and oubliettes. The poet Villon, imprisoned by the bishop in the summer of 1461 in the tower resting on the steeple of the church of St Liphard was pardoned by Louis XI, passing through Meung. ▲

BEAUGENCY stands on the Loire, its keep dating from the early twelfth century. Its foundations, separated from the motte which surrounds it, is made of blocks measuring 1 metre by 1.30 metres, originating from Roman monuments. 36 m high, 20 m per side, walls 3.80 m thick at the base, and 1.80 m at the top, linked to the castle by a drawbridge, it forms, with the castle, a fortress protected by a double curtain wall. Entrance is through a single door. The private kingdom was bought by Philip the Fair in 1291. Charles V gave it as a privilege to his son Louis d'Orléans. Beaugency suffered five sieges by the English during the Hundred Years' War. Joan of Arc regained the fortress in 1429. Charles d'Orléans gave the town to his half-brother, Dunois, who built, near the keep, the castle which bears his name. ▼

MONTIGNY-LE-GANNELON, an ancient small fortress of t twelfth century, saw its castle demolished in the fifteenth centu and rebuilt at the end of the same century, under the reign Louis XII, with a bond of brick and stone, popular at that tin The façade overlooking the Loir was restored in the nineteer century. The castle, well-furnished, offers the visitor interesti art collections. ▼

CHAMEROLLES, in the forest of Orléans, with its many streams and ponds filling its moats with water, is formed by three wings, four corner towers and a powerful square fort with adjacent turrets. The castle bears the stamp of the reign of Louis XII with its two-tone brickwork and above all the gallery leading into the left wing, similar to that of the castle of Blois of which, in fact, Lancelot du Lac, lord there, directed the works for the King. The Renaissance gardens have been successfully reinstated. ▲

▼ SAINT-BRISSON, a 12th century building, originally belonged to the Courtenay family. King Louis VI (*le Gros*) was received here in 1135, and King Philip Augustus in 1181. The structure forms a hexagon with a tower at each corner. The Lords of the Manor were the Clèves family, followed by the Séguier family (17th century). The castle was bequeathed to the town council in 1987, and became a venue for art exhibitions and events. Reconstructed mediaeval siege engines are operated every summer.

CHATEAUNEUF-SUR-LOIRE. The rotunda and a few outbuildings escaped, after the Revolution, the destruction of the very important castle, founded by the first Capetians and then included by Philip VI in the privilege of Orléans. This castle, sold by Louis XIV after 1646, was repurchased in 1653 by the secretary of state Phelypeaux and rebuilt.

CHATEAUDUN

In Gallic "dun" meant escarpment, hill and later fortress. The name of the castle bears witness to its ancient origins, as it overlooks the Loir valley from its rock. The first fortress mentioned is the one which Thibaud-le-Tricheur rebuilt in the early tenth century after the Normans came to wreak havoc, carried by the waterways as far as the heart of the country and towns. For four centuries, Chateaudun is to be one of the bases of the

powerful Counts of Blois. In 1391, Louis d'Orléans, brother of Charles VI, bought from Guy II of Châtillon the earldoms of Blois and Dunois, thus advantageously completing his dukedom of Orléanais. After his murder by his uncle Jean-Sans-Peur, Duke of Burgundy, Blois, Orléans and Châteaudun came to his son Charles who embarked on a campaign against the Burgundians and the English. On 25 October 1415, he was taken by the English at the Battle of Azincourt. He waited 25 years in England for his ransom to be paid. In 1439, during the final negotiations before his release, in which his half-brother took part, the famous bastard of Orléans, Charles gave him the earldom of Dunois; "the kind bastard" as Joan of Arc called him, became "Dunois" and received the reward for all the battles fought since the age of fifteen, for forty years, to defend Orléanais, and support the dauphin against the Burgundians and English. Dunois, from 1451 until his death in 1468, rebuilt the castle. He was by then one of the important figures of the kingdom, owning the earldoms of Dunois, Longueville, Gien, the estates of Beaugency, Montreuil-Bellay, Parthenay and many others. He preserved the circular keep built at the end of the twelfth century by Thibaud V. 31 metres high, with a diameter of 17 metres, it is typical of its kind: of the three superposed halls, the first two are arched with a dome, with a covered way made in the interior space between the foot of the vault and the floor of the upper storey. The door, 10 metres from ground level, opens into the covered way above the low hall and is to be found at present in the attic of the chapel. The second storey is not vaulted. A fine 15th-century framework adorns the top. The low hall took light in through a small opening, the one in the middle had three narrow windows, later widened and the upper one, three gemeled windows. A spiral staircase, in the thickness of the wall, led, from the entrance, into the upper rooms, another narrower one led from the upper hall to the crenellated top, once open. The entrance to the low hall was through a manhole in the vault, from the middle hall, near the well.

The Dunois wing, over the Loir, to the west, was built from 1459 to 1469, on three storeys and two underground levels (cellars, kitchens and dungeons). The dados and high walls follow the shape of the rock, retained in a springing momentum by the buttresses ending in turrets on the lofty covered way. The Norman architect Nicole Duval, in the service of Dunois, expressed, in language which is still that of the fifteenth century, a wish to live better and to transform fortresses into palaces. The sixteenth century and inspiration from Italy developed this trend in a different style, boosted by the ancient roots of a reviving art. A fine example of change, the large spiral staircase in the façade wall, with wide landings opening into a loggia, is

reminiscent of the staircase in the Louvre of Charles V, grandfather of Dunois, and is a foretaste of Renaissance staircases. Dunois, to show that he was a prince of royal blood, built a Holy Chapel next to the keep. This required the authorisation from the Pope and a relic of the Passion - in this case a fragment from the true Cross, a privilege reserved for royalty. The building includes two superposed chapels, two oratories and a square belltower. The statues, dating from the end of the fifteenth century, are of exceptional quality. The complex was built in several stages, the last one after the death of Dunois. François de Longueville, his son, finished the west wing and continued building of the northern one, taken over by François II de Longueville who succeeded him. The large staircase in this wing, inspired by that of the west wing, in several sections is a forerunner of the Francis I staircase in the castle of Blois.

LAVARDIN. Although the castle is vouched for towards the middle of the eleventh century, the first stone keep dates from 1070. At the end of the twelfth century, the lords of Lavardin added towers and tripled the facing: the fortress was the most secure in the Vendômois. Richard the Lionheart, who had taken Troo and Montoire, failed at Lavardin. In the fourteenth and fifteenth centuries, the castle was adapted for new strategies. In 1590 Henry IV had the fortress besieged by Conti for three weeks, dislodged part of the members of the League and demolished it.

LA POSSONNIERE. Louis de Ronsard, son of an officer of the forest of Gastine, gentleman of the mansion of Louis XII, knighted during the Italian campaigns, rebuilt the manor in 1515, a simple and charming residence, influenced by Italian taste and the humanist spirit, as can be seen from the mottos on the façades. Pierre de Ronsard was born there on 11 September 1524. He spent his childhood there, a pupil of his uncle Jean, parish priest of Bessé-sur-Braye.

BLOIS

As early as the ninth century, mention was made of a castle in Blois. It is probably this castle, which Thibaud le Tricheur, Count of Blois, who owned Tours and Chartres, fitted out and rebuilt in the middle of the tenth century. For 250 years the Counts kept their fiefs, adding Champagne to them. In 1230 the inheritance was handed over to the Châtillon family who continued the conversion of the castle. Froissard, historian of the fourteenth century, said that it was one of the finest places in the kingdom. Guy de Châtillon sold the earldom of Blois in 1391 to Duke Louis d'Orléans, who was assured, during this turbulent age, of a solid strategic base. After his assassination (1407) by a henchman of the Duke of Burgundy, his widow, Valentine de Milan, retired to Blois and died there. The young Duke, Charles, was still at battle with the troops of the Armagnacs, until the day of the defeat at Azincourt, 25 October 1415, when he was taken prisoner by the English. He was to remain a prisoner for 25 years in England, without the King paying his ransom, with poetry, an art in which he excelled, as only remedy for his boredom. When he returned in 1440, at the age of 46, he tried in vain to regain his place in the game of politics. The Duke, surrounded by a court of litterati, retired in 1450 to his castle in Blois which he fitted out and made more pleasant to live in, although we have no evidence of this since his successors had covered up his works with their own. He dedicated his life to art, to poetry, and to love: widower of Isabelle de France in 1407, of Bonne d'Armagnac in 1434, whom he grieved in several poems, he married, on his return, Marie de Clèves, a learned princess aged 14, who gave him a daughter, Marie, in 1445, and son, Louis, in 1462, who was to be King. The Duke and Duchess organised in Blois poetry games in which everyone could take part. Often a theme was given, a first verse, which had to be completed in a ballad or rondeau. François Villon, seeking adventure in the Orléans area, came to the court of Blois and participated with this decasyllable:

"I die of thirst before the fountain ....."

so that we have, on the same theme, the ballads of two great poets of the age, one a prince and one a crook. The Prince died in Blois in 1465.

His son, Louis, brought up at the castle, had made it his main residence when, the night of 7 to 8 April 1498, several messengers arrived from Amboise at a gallop: Charles VIII had

In the foreground on the left, the State Room, and the façade of the loggias, to the right and at right angles, the pavilions surrounding the Gaston d'Orléans wing, in the middle distance, the Louis XII wings and the St-Calais chapel, the square and the terrace, on the left, came within the boundaries of the original fortress.

Right-hand page: the façade of the loggias and Francis I by Clouet.

just died without an heir, thus Louis d'Orleans became Louis XII. With the crown he also received the hand of Queen Anne, the widow of the former King. He was to remain faithful to Blois. After his succession, he closed the sites of Amboise, the masters of the works Colin Biart and Jacques Sourdeau, the masons and stonecutters beeing summoned to Blois. Louis did not intend innovating but instead building, in the grounds of the old castle, a new royal residence, like at Amboise: a vast manor, more than a castle, open and airy, like the houses of merchants and officers of the town, without towers or battlements, with three brick and stone wings and galleries with basket-handle arches leading to rooms and appartments. The decoration, at times inspired by Italian features, remains faithful to the late Gothic tradition. The main wing looks out onto the front courtyard, today a square and terrace, previously contained within the walls. The pleasing façade, with its varied openings, its carriage and pedestrian entrances, retains the simplicity of which Louis XII was fond. On the main courtyard side it is flanked by two spiral staircase towers and opens on one side into the state room, a large lordly room of the castle of the Counts, and on the other side into the wing known as Charles d'Orléans, but definitely attributable to Louis XII, an elegant gallery resting on the chancel of the Saint-Calais chapel, consecrated in 1507. The nave was destroyed, like the end of the wing, in the seventeenth century. All of these buildings, in the same style, were constructed over some ten years. On the site of the Gaston d'Orléans wing, on the other side of the courtyard, stood a pretty building backing onto the ramparts, perched on a terrace with the name "Breton Perch", possibly because assigned,

under Louis XII, to the household of Queen Anne of Brittany which numbered gentlemen and ladies from this region. Linked to the castle by a gallery spanning the small valley, immense gardens, much admired by visitors of the time, covered the promontory, rising in tiers and embellished by covered galleries and pavilions of which the pavilion of Anne of Brittany (now the tourist office) remains as an example. Louis XII died in 1515, his sons dying at birth, so that his young cousin François d'Angoulême, who had married his daughter Claude the previous year, succeeded to the throne. From the first half of 1515, alteration works began on the castle of Blois and lasted until July 1524. On the courtyard side, the façade stands out on account of its novelty: no more brick alternating with stone, but instead large surfaces of light-coloured stone and an attempt at symmetry of which the architects of Louis XII were unaware. This symmetry is neither absolute nor systematic and the parts to the right and left of the staircase, previously equal in length, differ in the cadence of their openings, of the pillars which divide them vertically, and the panel ornaments. This is due to the fact that this façade was not applied to new buildings but to two separated buildings, with different levels, backing onto the curtain wall. The famous spiral

Page 24, the Francis I wing and staircase; in the corner, the State Room; on the right-hand page, below, the Louis XII wings and the St-Calais chapel.

On the right-hand page, above, the Louis XII wing and the State Room, exterior façades.

staircase, in an octagonal turret ornamented with openwork, joins these two halves, similar in idea to Gothic staircases, but innovating with its clerestory openings and theatrical role: this is a show staircase, made to see and to be seen. The abundant decoration, inspired by Florence and Milan, is still French in execution. On the town side, the thickness of the wall was doubled around 1520 in front of the curtain wall which separates the two adjacent buildings by a loggia façade which is reminiscent of the ducal palace in Urbino and Bramante's Vatican loggias. Two sites can be seen: the left part is characterised by the regular alternation of loggias and niches, while the right side does not have this regularity. The strange thing is that the French masons have reproduced the design but not the technical idea, having built a thick wall which they then perforated with deep concave walled loggias, creating the illusion of real arcades. In July 1524 Queen Claude died. The King left immediately for the Milan area: he was defeated and taken prisoner in Pavia in February 1525. He virtually never returned to Blois, nor did his architects. The castle was later the venue for festivals, love stories, endless dramas and intrigues which marked the reigns of Henry II and Catherine de Médicis, of the three kings, their children, and more particularly that of Henry III. In the large room of the former Counts of Blois, Henry III, in 1577, gathered the States General. The League, the Guise party, outmatched the King, in spite of the advice and manoeuvres of his mother, Catherine de Médicis, and war broke out again against the Huguenots.

Then there were the States General of 16 October 1588, when the King's speech ended with such a distinct threat against the League that a bloody outcome seemed inevitable.

This was the third act: on 23 December 1588, in the morning, the King summoned Guise to his appartment for confidential advice. He was told to return to the old studio, to which a dark passage led, and killers assassinated him. On Christmas day, the King again had killed, horribly, the Cardinal de Lorraine, brother of the Duke.

The Queen Mother, who had been ill, died on account of the double sin of her favourite son. On 30 July 1589, Henry III, who was preparing to crush Paris, was stabbed in Saint-Cloud by the monk Clément.

Henry IV had great plans for Blois which he was unable to fulfil. Louis XIII and Anne of Austria stayed there in April and May 1616. Marie de Médicis, the scheming Queen Mother, was put under house arrest there from 1617 to 1619 and escaped, in spite of her large size, through a window. Finally her younger son, Gaston, eternal plotter, received from Louis XIII the privilege of Orléans with the earldom of Blois where he came to live with plans to rase the old castle and rebuild a huge palace to the designs of a young architect, François Mansart. Only the Gaston d'Orléans wing was built (and left unfinished), replacing the elegant loggia of Anne of Brittany. The works finished at the end of 1638, on the birth of Louis XIV.

Above, the State Room; below, the bedroom of Henry III.

The bedroom of Catherine de Médicis...

Following pages on the left; fireplace with salamander, the symbol of Francis I; on the right, above, the façade of the loggias; below, the castles of Talcy and Ménars.

...the study.

TALCY. In 1517, the Florentine Salviati, steward of Francis I, bought the estate. The lord of Beaugency gave him consent to fortify the castle, provided he laid no claim to seigneurial rights. It is surprising that this rich Italian did not build, like the bankers from Tours, an Azay or Chenonceau. Did he conserve or build the square keep, or line the courtyard with wings in the manner of Louis XII? What remains for us and his gallery are pleasant, but Talcy is renowned for its poets: Ronsard serenaded Cassandre, daughter of Salviati. Diane, niece of Cassandre, and the poet Agrippa d'Aubigné, Huguenot captain, loved each other but were separated by the religious wars. ▼

MENARS. The descendants of Charron, postmaster at Montlivault, owners of the castle and of the land since 1636 and made prosperous through important responsibilities under Louis XIV, expanded their property, which became one of the most important in Blésois. It was sold in 1759 to Madame de Pompadour, former official mistress of Louis XV and still his friend. She commissioned Gabriel to convert the castle. At her death in 1764, at the age of 43, her brother, Marigny, director of the King's buildings, inherited it. For him Soufflot completed the castle and redesigned the gardens leading to the Loire in vast terraces, opposite the ideal landscape of the valley, its fields and forests. ▼

The castle, from left to right: the north tower of the outer walls, the oratory of Francis I, the north galleries, the keep, north tower of the northwest façade, west tower, the galleries, the west tower of the outer walls, and in the foreground Cosson. Below: a salamander, emblem of Francis I.

CHAMBORD

The Counts of Blois had at "Chambourd", which in Gallic means "ford on the curve" (Dauzat dictionary), a fortified keep, known of since the twelfth century. They used it for war, lodging and hunting. There is still talk in Sologne of the ghostly hunt of Count Thibaud who rides by, on stormy nights, under the wild clouds...

The Dukes of Orléans succeeded the Counts of Blois, Louis d'Orléans became Louis XII and François d'Angoulême, his son-in-law, hunting in the forests of Boulogne and Chambord, often crossed, riding behind dogs and valets, the Cosson ford, at the foot of the old keep. The equipage stopped there to dine and lodge, after the quarry. He loved this landscape of forests, ponds and brooks, the heather and the thick brushwood where the animals hid.

When he succeeded Louis XII at the age of 20, he marked out his future by converting Blois, although it was at Chambord, in a vast, open area, in the middle of the woods, where he was to build the ideal royal residence which he had dreamed of for a long time, a sumptuous hunt meeting-place designed for gods or legendary kings, a romanesque and poetic place.

Several designs had already been produced for the young Prince who was keen on architecture, probably with his participation. Dominique de Cortone, Italian engineer and architect who had followed Charles VIII to France, had built a wooden model which seemed to herald the future keep of Chambord, but with a straight, more "modern" staircase. Leonardo da Vinci was no stranger to it, having worked on the design of a huge castle to be built at Romorantin. He had also designed several plans of spiral staircases with combined turns, in line with a building illuminated by a dome, as the Chambord staircase was to be by its lantern tower. Leonardo, although he could not take part directly in the design of Chambord (the site was opened in October 1519, four months after his death), did however influence the spirit of all his followers, particularly that of the young Prince.

The first site was assigned, in September 1519, to François de Pontbriand, as superintendent, and to Jacques Sourdeau as mason. Both had worked at Amboise and at Blois. First of all the old castle had to be demolished and then, on peaty and marshy ground, foundations 5 metres deep built on piles and embedded rocks.

Nicolas de Foyal took over the works in 1521, with Trinqueau, master mason. The Pavia disaster in 1525 stopped all expenditure (the ransom of the King, that of the hostages, Francis and Henry, his sons, were fixed by Charles V at 2 million gold crowns, of which 1 million two hundred thousand when the princes were freed: 4 tonnes of gold).

On his return in October 1526, Francis restarted building, with Charles de Chauvigny as superintendent, Forget as treasurer, and Trinqueau still as master mason. There were workmen on the site apparently until 1800. It was at this time that the King appeared to decide to develop the whole building.

The work extended, symbolically, from a square residence surrounded by round towers, a traditional form of keep, the heart of royal power which every seigneur exercised. The construction and proportions were modelled on strict mathematical rules and the theory of the golden section.

The keep: terrace and attic.
Below, the keep: entrance façade between the south towers, on the left, and east; on the right, the Francis I wing.

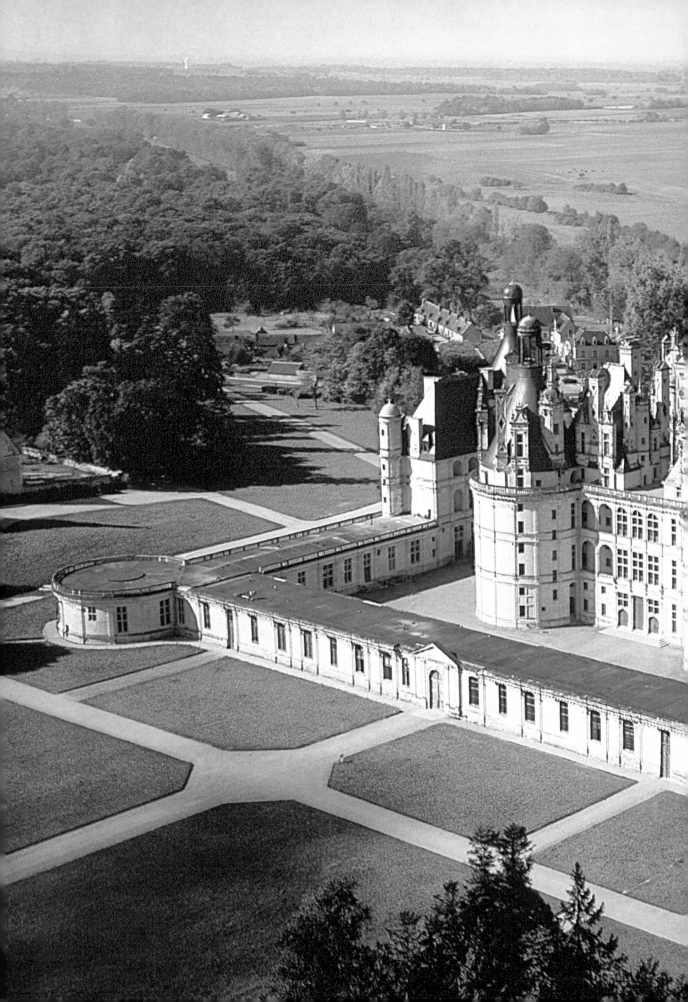

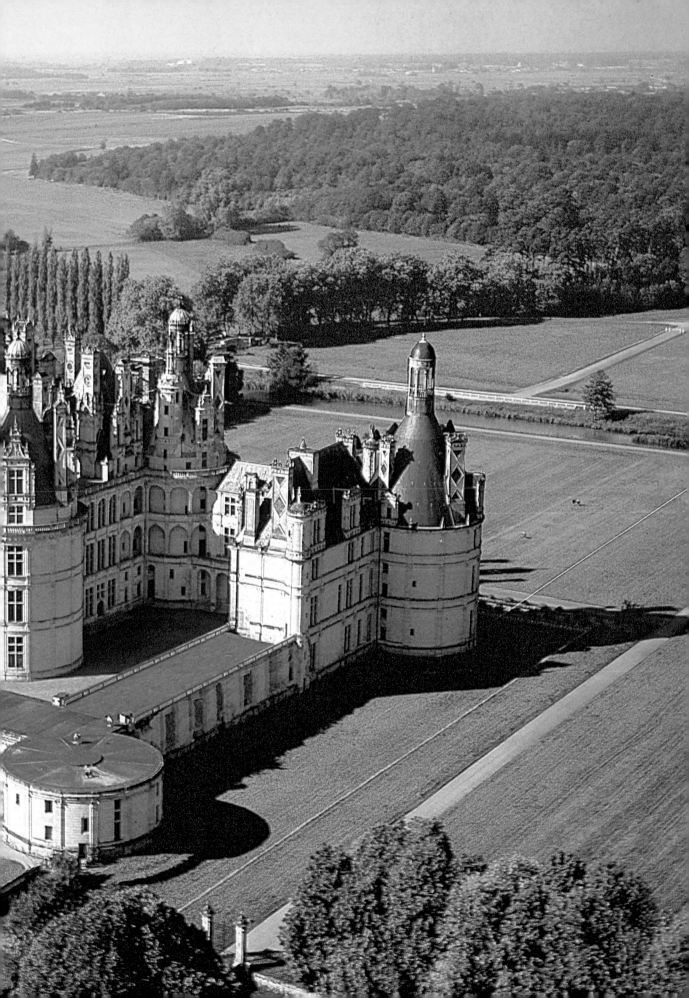

Previous double page: overall view of the castle, taken from the east: the towers and low wings and the royal gate; the keep; on the right the north tower of the outer walls and the Francis I wing; far left the symmetrical "Henry II" wing.
Above: northwest façade.
Opposite left: the staircase of the Francis I wing.

The axis of the keep is the splendid staircase whose two bricked spiral flights rise independently around a column with openings as far as the lantern tower. The sculpted decoration of the capitals, the consoles, niches, box vaults, are successfully united with the forms of the fifteenth century in France, still Gothic, and those of the fifteenth century in Italy, already classical.

These flights lead, without joining, to the four Greek-cross landings of the four sections of each storey of the keep. Each section forms a complete apartment, in the same way as each storey of the four corner towers, so that there are eight apartments on each level, those of the towers reached by a passage along the wall of the keep.

The thirty-two apartments are independent, composed of a large bedroom and outbuildings on the mezzanine, all with fireplaces, and those of the towers, with small spiral staircases. According to the custom introduced in the sixteenth century, the toilets are in the attic, to encourage necessary ventilation.

The three storeys of the keep are divided, in the Italian style, by superposed pillars decorating regularly the façade without necessarily corresponding to openings, and by double bands of friezes, in a regular pattern. A certain irregularity in the rhythm of the windows ensures a lively and unexpected look for the façades, which often enlivens the beauty of the shapes.

This ancient "Gothic" freedom, still rebelling against the symmetrical perfection which the Romans taught, is to be found in the fantastic town of steeples, towers, chimneys, lanterns which soar over the terrace, with its lead work formerly gilded with fine gold. We are reminded of the delicate and flamboyant apartments perched on towers and keeps of the painted castles in the "très riches heures" of the Duke of Berry. However the geometric slate inlays are reminiscent of Italy as well as the façades where the architect plays with the shapes and colours of the marbles.

Such was this keep, forming on its own a complete castle, which Charles V of Spain, passing through France, with the chivalrous permission of the King of France, to return to his Flemish towns, discovered in 1539, without concealing his wonder. Starting from the north and west towers of this keep, curtain walls join the north and west towers of the rectangular, 156 metre, outer walls, which close off the courtyard. The east and south towers are to remain low, according to a solution adopted from the fifteenth century onwards in certain castles such as Plessis-Bourré. The north tower of the outer walls and the apartments of Francis I, at right angles to the northeast curtain wall, were built starting from 1539 and, during the 'forties, linked to the keep by a gallery on the curtain wall. This part of the works was supervised by the widow of Jean Breton, lord of Villandry. At the same time the west tower of the outer wall and the southwest wing were begun, again linked to the keep. The staircases of Francis I, north tower, and of Henry II, west tower, were added independently, as was the oratory, positioned in the corner formed, outwards, by the north outer wall tower and the curtain wall at the start of a staircase which was to link the foot of the tower with the gallery. During the same period, the low wings of the outbuildings were built.

The earthenware stove of Marshal de Saxe.

The royal bedroom and its ceremonial bed, décor for the levee and going-to-bed ceremony according to protocol.

The gallery of paintings of the Duchess of Berry.

The bedroom of the Count of Chambord, in the foreground: the battery of miniature cannons, a souvenir of the Count's childhood.

The birth of the Count of Chambord (1820).

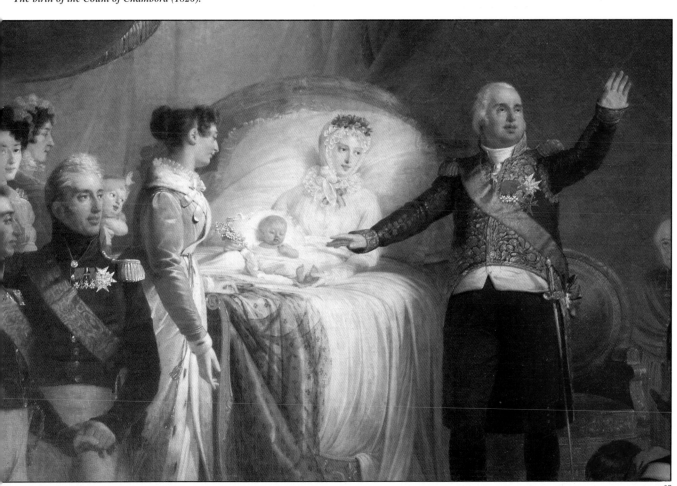

Bedroom of Francis I

The Queens bedroom

Life at Chambord consisted of periods of intense activity followed by long periods of total abandon. When the King arrived, the whole household preceeded him and followed him, all the ministers and officers of his governments, the household of the Queen, those of the princes. The royal caravan brought trunks, beds, hangings, tapestries, works of art, books, trestles, tables and chairs, all that was necessary, including the superfluous, for the private and public life of the King, of the court and government. The cartages of the suppliers arrived from the cities, towns and estates by all routes, since a whole town had to be immediately fed, watered, dressed, served and amused, when yesterday there were only a few officers, a worksite, a small village. Then there were the royal hunts which covered each day some area of the vast estate. When the court had departed again, the immense, deserted castle seemed abandoned for centuries; the woods and paths were empty and the traveller discovered, on his way, a marvellous palace, totally strange because it was empty, as if by a magic spell. Francis I came to Chambord for the last time in February-March 1545. For 18 years, the charms of Fontainebleau distracted this fickle monarch from those of the Loire valley. Perhaps he regretted not having fulfilled his plan: not having been able, among other things, to divert the Loire as far as the walls of the castle.

His son, Henry II, Catherine de Médicis and their children, including three kings, stayed there, above all for the hunting. The anecdote of Charles IX hunting down a stag without dogs has remained famous. Henry IV totally neglected the estate but his younger son, Gaston d'Orléans, often stayed there, coming from his house arrest at Blois, which led him to begin some essential restoration work. The court of Louis XIV moved there regularly from 1668 to 1685, and the great King had the west wing and attic covered. The first performances of "Monsieur de Pourceaugnac" and of the "Bourgeois Gentilhomme" by Molière and Lulli were given at Chambord.

The carriage of the Count of Chambord

Louis XV in 1725 hosted at Chambord for 8 years his father-in-law Stanislas Leszczynski, dethroned King of Poland and future last Duke de Lorraine, who cursed the unhealthy atmosphere of the neglected and very damp castle. From 1746, this same King offered the estate, as a retreat, to the Marshal Maurice de Saxe, who lodged his regiment there and conducted, sheltering in the royal residence, his tumultuous and unbridled love affair with the actress Adrienne Lecouvreur. He died there in 1750, in a somewhat bizarre fashion.

After having escaped the demolitioners during the Revolution, the castle was offered by Napoleon to Marshal Berthier and sold by his widow. It was bought by national subscription in 1821 for the son of the Duke of Berry, Henri, who became the Count of Chambord. When the royalists summoned him to the throne in 1871, this Prince made his candidacy unacceptable by rejecting the tricolour flag. No longer needed, the ceremonial carriages provided for his entry into Paris remained at the castle. The government bought Chambord in 1930.

The castle is today fully renovated, its moats, filled in during the eighteenth century, have been re-excavated and supplied with water from the Cosson brook. It is in perfect condition and state of repair which would probably surprise all those who had lived there. The crowd of tourists has replaced that of the court, walking along all the mazes of this universe which is both grandiose and familiar. Everyone can walk for hours there, discover new rooms, unexpected views, details to savour, walk along the terraces, look out over the gardens and woods, leaning over the balustrades, like those who followed, listening and watching, the progress of the royal hunts across the immense estate.

The castle conservation organisation keeps the building furnished, more completely than it has ever been. The royal apartments of the Francis I wing display again the décor of the builder Prince, his bedroom, the audience room, his study with the vault decorated with initials, lilies and salamanders, the animal symbolising King Francis.

The apartments of the keep evoke the sojourns of Louis XIV, of the Marshal de Saxe, of the Count of Chambord. A permanent exhibition is dedicated to hunting with fine collections loaned by the Museum of Hunting of the hôtel Guénégaud in Paris (Sommer foundation).

Chambord was in fact born from the hunt. The castle would have no meaning nor charm without the forests, the ponds, the streams and the plains where, on an area of 5,500 hectares, in a walled enclosure with a circumference of 33 km, stags, deers and wild boars live, a vast reservation of wild fauna. 1,000 hectares (the average surface area of a French village) are open to hikers who get to know the animals running wild from the observatories formed opposite the spaces bordered by woods, or walking, or riding on horseback, along the paths and roads of the kingdom.

Combining the perfection of Nature and the creation of Man, Chambord is both enchantment and logical beauty, inspiration and composition. The festivals and arts find there more than a setting, a mere décor, a possibility of accompaniment, a creative complicity and charm which make the concerts more pleasant and the shows more magical.

There are places where stupidity and mediocrity disappear, or almost: Chambord is one of these.

The bridge over the Cosson, built in 1708.

BEAUREGARD

In 1495, Louis, Duke of Orléans, future Louis XII, raised the land of Beauregard to seigneury for Jean Doulcet, a bourgeois from Blois, financier to the family of Orléans and conferred a title of nobility on him. The new lord, then his son François, built a manor, most likely resembling the constructions of Louis XII in Blois, and which can be seen on the engraving by Androuet du Cerceau of 1579.

Francis I bought the castle, possibly as a hunt meeting-place, and offered it in 1521 to his uncle and godfather, the Great Bastard of Savoy, killed at Pavia in 1525.

Jean du Thier, lord of Ménars, secretary of state to Henry II, bought the residence in 1545 for 2000 gold crowns. This friend of Ronsard, humanist and poet when the fancy took him, had a castle built of which the essential part has remained for us to see, with its central wing formed by a gallery on seven arcades, of which the ground floor remains open, bearing a storey with three windows framed by pillars, extending those of the arcades, the whole with an attic having three large windows decorated with niche pediments, in the style of the second Renaissance. On either side of the gallery there are two pavilions, linked to two parallel buildings. On the first floor of the left-hand pavilion, du Thier set up, in 1554, his study, fully panelled including the coffered ceiling, with sculpted and gilded oak, the work of Scibec de Carpi, creator, among other things, of the panelling in the Francis I gallery at Fontainebleau. The small bells, repeated everywhere, are those of the coat of arms of du Thier: light blue with three golden bells. Allegorical paintings in the pannelling refer to human activities, the work of Niccolo del'Abbate or his workshop. The fireplace was added in the seventeenth century. The perfection of the whole recalls the famous trompe-l'oeil closet by Botticelli at the palace in Urbino.

On the death of du Thier in 1559, the castle came into the hands of Florimont II Robertet, who succeeded him in his work.

In 1619 Paul Ardier, great servant to the crown, under Henry IV and Louis XIII, (he was controller general of la Gabelle, then treasurer of l'Epargne) bought the private kingdom. Although he had the old Doulcet building destroyed, which is possibly regrettable, he did build the gallery of illustrious figures, which houses, in twelve panels dedicated to twelve reigns, from Philip VI to Louis XIII, 327 portraits of kings, queens, princes, popes, cardinals, great captains, great writers, scholars and others who were famous in their day, painted by Jean Mosnier of Blois, according to old documents. The panelling and ceiling are also decorated with scenes allegories, devices and ornamental patterns. The floor is entirely tiled with Delft images of an army on the march, each tile representing a figure. Today the castle belongs to the Count and Countess du Pavillon who have brought together rare collector's items: furniture, tapestries and objets d'art. The original kitchen, in perfect state of repair, can also be visited.

Left-hand page, top, the façade overlooking the park. Until the nineteenth century, the central gallery was set back in relation to the side pavilions. The doubling of this gallery placed it at the same level.
At the side, a Dutch clock by Antson Fette (eighteenth century).
Below: ceiling of the "Grelots" studio.
Above: gallery of famous personages.
Opposite: detail of the Delft tiles.
Below: entrance façade.

CHEVERNY

There is mention in the archives of the old Blésois family of the Huraults, from the end of the thirteenth century. Ennobled by Philip VI de Valois, the family owned, from 1340 to 1812, the land of Saint-Denis-sur-Loire, one league upriver from Blois. In 1504 Jacques Hurault, the younger son, having performed high financial and administrative functions under Louis XI, Charles VIII and Louis XII, acquired the seigneury of Cheverny. His son, Raoul, obtained permission from Louis XII to build a fortress there; finance general under Francis I, he narrowly escaped the purge which the King had carried out in the realms of his financiers and creditors. The most powerful of these, Beaune de Semblançay, whose daughter had married Raoul, was ignobly hanged on Monfaucon gallows. Raoul Hurault went to war in Italy and was killed under the walls of Naples. His widow, most likely ruined, like most of the families of the bankers implicated in this exemplary affair, sold Cheverny to a chaplain of Henry II, who sold it in turn in 1551 to the royal mistress, Diane de Poitiers. Diane remained owner until 1565, then accepted to sell it again to the son of Raoul Hurault. The estate fell to Philippe Hurault, Count of Cheverny, governor of Orléanais and of Chartres then chancellor of France under Henry III, then Henry IV. Until his death in 1599 he was one of the most loyal and consulted counsellors of the first Bourbon King. In the history of the first ten years of the reign there is mention everywhere of Cheverny. His son, Henri, bailiff and governor of Blois, general lieutenant in the government of Orléanais, had married a Miss Chabot who was unfaithful to him. Caught in the act, the Countess was forced to poison herself and the guilty equerry was executed without trial. This was possibly the reason why Henri also had the castle, the scene of the crime, eliminated.

His second wife, Marguerite Gaillard de la Morinière, a neighbouring estate, was apparently the instigator behind the building of the present castle.

Around 1625, the direction of the site was assigned to Jacques Bougier, master mason, known for his works at Blois. In 1629 the German sculptor and carpenter Hammerber supplied the frames. The construction of the buildings ended in 1634. Marguerite died in 1635 and Henri in 1648. Their daughter Elisabeth, Marquess of Montglas, continued the decoration of the apartments admired by the architect Félibien and the daughter of Gaston d'Orléans, la Grande Mademoiselle, neighbour of Cheverny, whether in Blois or in Chambord. Louis de Clermont, son of the Marquess, took no interest in the property which he left to his cousin Clermont d'Amboise, heavily engaged in a military career and little concerned with dealing with the considerable expenditure which the repair of the castle required, according to a detailed estimate of 1724. He sold it to Count d'Harcourt, lieutenant general of Blésois. The health of the Countess forced her to live in Switzerland and the Count considered selling his office and Cheverny. Dufort, heir of a family of magistrates and receiver of a large fortune, had obtained from Louis XV the post of initiator of embassies, an important position, in the service of the minister for foreign affairs. With the invaluable support of Madame de Pompadour, known and appreciated by him, in 1764 he obtained permission from the King to buy from d'Harcourt the post of lieutenant general of Blésois, at the same time as the land, and to take the title of Count of Cheverny. He found the castle to be in the hands of a steward, in a state of decay, but with the cultivated land sown with wheat up to the staircase steps, the castle only having a total of five inhabitable rooms. He decided to restore the castle to a fit state and to refurbish a pavilion per winter "there were five of them, this means five years' work ...." he wrote.

However it took him twelve years to make this castle once again "one of the most comfortable in the province..." A man of wit, lover of the theatre, of literature and music, he gave at Cheverny, with his wife, children and friends, wonderful receptions and enjoyed the company of his numerous relations from Paris and the provinces. His simplicity, understanding and the care he always took not to offend anybody, at the same time earning respect, enabled him to survive the Revolution and terror, saving his life and the castle, although arrested and imprisoned for some time at Blois. He sold the estate in 1799 on the death of his son. In 1825 Cheverny was bought by Anne Denis Hurault, Marquis of Vibraye, of the elder branch. He filled in the moats to the south and demolished the eighteenth-century outbuildings. Since that time the castle has always remained in the family.

Above: the castle, south façade, and its outbuildings.
Below: the pack in the kennels. The stag in the pond.
Right-hand page: above, the dining-room; below, the Téniers tapestry room, the King's bedroom.
Pages 48, 49: The staircase - The fireplace in the large drawing-room, decorated with the portrait of Marie-Johanne de la Carre Saumery, Countess of Cheverny, painted by Mignard - The equipage.

The Marquis Philippe Hurault de Vibraye, who died in 1976, was one of the first owners in France to understand the need to open historical residences to the public at the same time continuing to live there and maintaining its traditions, French hunting for example, a royal passion and subtle art in practice where, according to a commonly accepted ritual, all levels of society come together. The visit to the kennels of 70 hunting hounds in the pack, a cross between foxhounds and Poitevins, and to the trophy room where the horns of around 2,000 stags are displayed, bear witness to the vitality of the equipage of Cheverny since 1850.

The inventory of fixtures of 1724 and the memoirs of Dufort tell us that the castle was similar to the one we see today, with a few differences however. Its overall plan marks a complete break with the idea of the feudal castle, as if "corrected" by the Renaissance. Cheverny is mentioned as the first example of this style of the seventeenth century which is later to be called "classical". The layout of the fortified castle has not however disappeared. The narrower central pavilion, which bears the coat of arms of the lord and contains the staircase with its two straight and vaulted flights, reminds us of the entrance fort, the two side pavilions, higher and more powerful, correspond to the intermediary towers and pavilions of the curtain walls. Even more medieval are the moats, filled in during the nineteenth century on the south side but preserved in the north. Their design is echoed by that of the border. However there is no longer a keep or crenellations, nor machicolations. As for the décor, it no longer has the invention and imagination of the old Gothic genius, to the benefit of a

wholly Roman architectural austerity. The balance of the volumes and the symmetry are those of an ideal working drawing. The relief and spirit of the south façade are born of quality and working of the materials, the stone of Bourré, hard limestone which whitens with age. There is no question of a transformation into leaf patterns, figures or animals: stone is still stone. The master worker plays with the lines and shadows in cutting it into horizontal joint lines over the whole width of the façade, adding to it a double block of figures between the floors. This powerful and understated composition is decorated with rounded niches, adorned with the busts of the twelve Caesars, the arched pediments of the ground floor, in facing scrolls, at the storeys, and the regular pattern of the high superposed windows. The space of the main courtyard, at that time fully paved, was bordered by moats and, on both sides, to the left, by a gallery and to the right by a wall perforated with thirteen openings, forming two wings leading to the two large pavilions just before they join the central

façade, which accentuated their appearance of towers and created attractive perspective and proportions. The north façade is treated in a different fashion, in a common style under Louis XIII, in stone anchorages, framing rubble stone masonry, previously coated. To the north of the park, the fine orangery of the eighteenth century faces south. The true sights of Cheverny begin with a visit to the apartments: ceilings, wood panelling, fireplaces, painted by the Blésois Jean Mosnier who had worked for Marie de Médicis at the Luxembourg palace, also decorator of Ménars, Valençay and Beauregard, wood panelling by Hammerber, high quality pieces of furniture, tapestries, from sketches by Vouet or Téniers, portraits painted by Clouet, Rigaud and Mignard, paintings attributed to Titian and to Raphael. The whole, still in place, gives the visitor the sensation of being received in its residence by the Hurault family .... which is not far from the truth since the castle is still in effect inhabited by the descendants of this ancient lineage.

Above: the armory decorated by Mosnier; Gobelins tapestry (1621); the Abduction of Helen after François Franck, an Antwerp painter.
Below: Small drawing-room with tapestries, "Bowls Players" by Téniers (17th century Flanders).

Fireplace in the armory room, supported by caryatids; on the decorative panel: The Death of Adonis by Jean Mosnier on one side and on the other, Mercury, Venus and Cupid, two cherubs.

LE MOULIN (opposite, page 53). Charles d'Angoulême, lord of Romorantin, father of Francis I, in 1490 authorised the equerry Philippe d Moulin to fortify his residence of Lassay-sur-Croisne, which was being built. This equerry, a few years later in 1495, saved Charles VI during the battle won at Fornoue. The King arranged an extremely convenient marriage with the widow of Jean d'Harcourt, made hi chamberlain and advisor, entrusting him with the government of Langres, where he died in 1506.

Building of the castle began around 1480, in bricks decorated with diamond shapes, with stone anchorages, it has all the attributes of fortress: entrance fort, drawbridge, wide moats, four machicolation corner towers of which only one remains. However the material and th walls show that these are symbolic attributes; the loggia, typical of seigneurial residences of the end of the fifteenth century, stands on thr levels; a spiral staircase, in a square tower, leads to the apartments: two rooms per floor and an outhouse, in the round half-tower supporte by the outer façade. At the foot of the loggia, a delicate flamboyant oratory.

CHEVERNY, above: Flanders tapestry (17th century), Téniers cartoon, "The Return of the Fishermen"; below: the trophy room.

TROUSSAY. This manor, built in the 15th century in the district of Cheverny and decorated in the 16th century, was restored by architect La Morandière for historian L. de la Saussaye of the Institut de France, who inherited it in 1828. La Saussaye embellished it with rare antique decorations from villas and castles like Bury Castle, which were destined to disappear. Troussay, which is inhabited and exquisitely furnished, combines the elegance of the Loire Valley residences with the family charm of the rural property of Sologne, evoked by a fascinating regional museum housed in the huge outbuildings.
◀

FOUGERES. A very ancient Blésois seigneury, mentioned from 1030, it was bought in 1334 by Gaucher de Faverois who was with the Duke d'Orléans. In 1356 the Black Prince captured the castle and left it in ruins, except for the keep. Charles VII regained it in 1429, on leaving for Rheims. Jeanne-de-Faverois in 1438 married Pierre de Refuge, ducal advisor who served Charles VII and Louis XI in the highest financial offices. The latter authorised him to rebuild the castle. At a time when open and non-fortified residences were already being built at Blois, Loches and Amboise to make life pleasant, situated nevertheless within strong walls, Pierre de Refuge, like at the same time Jean Bourré at Langeais, built a fortress for the war, which he no longer knew. Even without its moats, filled in and once supplied with water from the brook of Bièvre, it remains a model of military architecture of the fifteenth century, with the memory of the original square keep, whose base dates back to the eleventh century. ▶

VILLESAVIN. Jean Breton, captured at Pavia with Francis I, took possession of the land of Villesavin on his return from captivity in 1527. His post as head of the treasury at Blois led him to deal with the financing of the sites of Chambord, for which his widow was to take effective responsibility. He began Villesavin in 1527 and in 1528, having become lord of Villandry, he had the castle there rebuilt. It is thought that decoration of Villesavin continued until 1537. The design of this "very modern" residence is that of an Italian villa. The square pavilions replace the towers in the old style, doors, windows and skylights are decorated with much talent and invention, nothing remains of the military and seigneurial fittings of the old castles. ▼

CHAUMONT

The inner courtyard of which the north wing disappeared in the eighteenth century.

In the tenth century, Eudes I, Count of Blois, and Foulques Nerra, Count of Anjou, contested the Loire valley. Eudes, from his tower at Chaumont, halfway between Amboise and Blois, set up a watch over the banks of the Loire, the plain as far as Cher, the Beuvron valley. One of the vassals of Blois, Gelduin, a Norman knight, fought with the Count at the siege of Langeais. The same Gelduin served Eudes II, son of the former, but lost Saumur which Foulques regained. Gelduin returned to his fief of Pontlevoy and received from the Count the fortress of Chaumont.

His son, Geoffroy Puella, "the girl", without heirs, gave Chaumont to a son of Denise de Fougères, his sister, and of Sulpice d'Amboise. Chaumont thus came into the d'Amboise family. Hugues d'Amboise, second lord of Chaumont, built a stone keep there, the same as at Montrichard, forming a mighty triangle: Amboise, Chaumont and Montrichard.

In the twelfth century, Thibaud V of Blois demolished the castle of Sulpice II which his son rebuilt. During the thirteenth century Chaumont, according to alliances, passed from father to son, or daughter, sometimes nephew.

In the fourteenth century the elder branch kept Amboise, and Chaumont fell to the younger branch with the name of Chaumont d'Amboise. Peter I was born of this branch, compromised in the rebellion of the Greats against Louis XI, know as the "league of public good". The King had Chaumont demolished and burnt, and confiscated the land. Shortly afterwards he gave his pardon and authorised the rebuilding, which Peter undertook, and contributed towards it. The clemency of Louis XI was fortunate: Peter I, who died in 1473, had by Anne de Bueil, his wife, 17 children who provided the élite of the servants to the Crown, the Church and the arts, during the reigns of Charles VIII, Louis XII and Francis I.

Charles I, the elder, continued the rebuilding of the north and west wings, from 1473 to 1475. Among his brothers, Louis, bishop of Albi, fitted out the chancel of his cathedral, Pierre II, bishop of Poitiers, built the castle of Dissay, Jacques, abbot of Cluny, built the famous hôtel de Cluny in Paris, Georges, the youngest, born in Chaumont in 1460, and the most famous, later bishop of Montauban, archbishop of Narbonne and Rouen, and perpetual legate cardinal to the Pope, was a friend of Louis XII and the first of his ministers. A builder like his brothers, around 1510 he led in France the fashion of the Renaissance spirit with the Norman castle of Gaillon.

When his nephew, Charles II, successor to Charles I, in 1501 had to abandon the castle to take over the general lieutenancy of Milan, the cardinal moved into Chaumont and directed the works which he evidently dealt with briskly, because he received Louis XII and the court in the summer of 1503. Charles d'Amboise stayed less on the Loire than in his Milanese government. He died there in 1511, at the age of 38. Georges d'Amboise, his son, was killed at Pavia in 1525 at the age of 22.

The castle, through the women, stayed in the family until 1550. Catherine de Médicis then bought it for 120,000 livres. After the death of Henry II, on 9 July 1559, she demanded to Diane de Poitiers, the favourite, the restitution of Chenonceau, but gave her Chaumont in return. Diane, extremely interested, did not lose out: the income from Chaumont was much higher than that of Chenonceau. Diane, through her arrogance, had the covered way, the crenellations and machicolations rebuilt, which she then decorated with her monogram and emblems. She stayed there little, preferring Anet where she died in 1566.

The castle later fell into the hands of owners from the world of banking, parliament and business. In the eighteenth century, Nicolas Bertin de Vauguyen opened the fortress on the Loire by demolishing the north wing. Under Louis XV, le Ray, from Nantes, great master of the Waterways and Forests, installed in the outbuildings a glassworks and ceramic and pottery factory, where famous artists worked, including an Italian from Urbino, J. B. Nini, engraver on glass and specialist of terracotta medallion portraits. The fashion was for medallions and profiles, from miniatures to calligraphy, via the silhouette. He achieved great success. The castle had a collection of these medallions, including several of Franklin, linked to Le Ray whose son handled interests in America, in particular those of Necker and Madame de Staël, his daughter. The latter, banned from the region of Paris by Napoleon, moved in for several months in 1810, with a whole set of intellectuals, at the home of the young Le Ray, who was in America at the time.

Under the Restoration, the Baron d'Etchegoyen, the Count d'Aramon and Viscount Walsh were owners. Walsh commissioned the architect J. de la Morandière to restore the west wing (reconstruction of a gable over the Loire) and of the façade overlooking the courtyard of the south wing, which had been "modernised" in the eighteenth century.

Above, the west wing with its square tower, the overhanging keep, the south wing.

Opposite left: a suit of armour from the sixteenth century;
on the right: French chest from the sixteenth century and Flemish tapestry "The Judgement of Paris" (16th-century).

Right-hand page, above: the dining-room and the fireplace designed by Sanson (end of the nineteenth century), on the right a detail of this fireplace with, to the right, the coat of arms of Charles d'Amboise, and to the left that of Charles II.

Centre left: the harness room; right: the stable yard.

Below: the massive entrance fort; the large drawbridge is lowered and raised again each day.

The last era of Chaumont makes it original compared to the castles of the Loire valley. It began in 1875 when Mademoiselle Say, one of the two daughters of the extremely wealthy sugar producer, bought the estate and married Prince Amédée de Broglie. The Princess commissioned the architect Sanson to transform Chaumont into a luxury residence.

The park was created by Henri Duchêne; the church perched on the northeastern slope, and the hamlets built near the castle were moved to the bank of the Loire, the interiors fitted out, restoring a décor in the neo-Medieval style, with the addition of furniture, hangings, paintings and objets d'art bought all over Europe at high prices, with above all a considerable increase in comfort and which does not spread to society, even the well-off society, until several decades later. The horses were also given the same modernisation treatment: the stables built by Sanson on the site of the former outbuildings, a wonder of luxury and organisation, give a glimpse behind the scenes of the princely life

at Chaumont, whose receptions were the main topic of social gossip. All this splendour, with the death of the Prince, the remarriage of the Princess with a great and lavish lord and the depression of 1929 ran the Princess out of her fortune. The government bought the castle in 1938 with 17 hectares of parkland. The 2483 hectares of land, woods and vineyards of the estate had already been sacrificed. The castle, in spite of the disappearance of the north wing, gives a good idea of one of the last seigneurial fortresses: the d'Amboise tower in the west which serves as a keep, and the west wing, are the oldest parts, the north wing having disappeared. The square tower, in the middle of the wing, ensures complete cover by the fire of the defenders. The south wing and the entrance offer traditional defences, the east wing, from a later date, does not have a tower in the middle of the curtain wall. However the ornamentation, the two decorative friezes which circle the two tiers of the castle, the covered way of Diane de Poitiers and the octagonal staircase tower of the courtyard, all mark the change from the late Gothic style to the Italian influence and from the fortress to the country palace. La Morandière and Sanson have left a fine anthology of the era of restorers, started by Viollet-le-Duc and Mérimée.

AMBOISE

The strategic position of the plain, platform for the castle, has interested Man since his arrival on the banks of the great river. Amboise was an important site, from prehistoric times up to the eras of the Celts, Romans and to modern times.

In the eleventh century, three lords in their three keeps, all three at Amboise, engaged, along the route of the Loire, an endless war, vassals of the Counts of Blois or of Anjou.

In 1106, Hugues, vassal of Blois, gained possession of the fief. It is reasonable to imagine at this time a powerful castle like Loches or Chinon. It dominated the Loire, the island and the bridge. This is the start of the Amboise dynasty which is to hold power until Charles VII, influenced by the devious La Trémoïlle, accused Louis d'Amboise of treason and confiscated the fortress and the estate, now once again under the crown.

Charles VII stayed there occasionally - he may have begun a loggia; in any case Louis XI commissioned major works there, both to improve the fortifications and to set up an adequate residence for the Queen, Charlotte of Savoy, and her children, including the dauphin Charles, who was born there in 1470. The future Charles VIII spent his childhood there, under the supervision of Jean Bourré, whom the King trusted. The village of Amboise, at the foot of the fortress, was so small that no traveller could stay there, the parish was in any case off-limits to outsiders, so great was the King's fear for his heir, of plague and intrigues,

or any other stroke of fate, so that the Court of Amboise was lacking in life and brilliance. As for Louis XI, he preferred staying in Tours, or, always on horseback, he toured his estates.

In spite of this Charles VIII remained very attached to the place of his childhood. When he became king, away from the regency of his sister, Anne de Beaujeu, he undertook with enthusiasm the rebuilding of the loggias and defences. The Florentine ambassadors wrote that it was more a town than a castle. It was Amboise which featured the names of the master masons Colin Biart, Guillaume Senault, Louis Armanjeart, Pierre Trinqueau, Jacques Sourdeau .... who later worked on the other sites of the Loire valley. Engaged in the costly campaigns in Italy which were to ruin the peninsula and the kingdom of France, Charles VIII did however bring back the taste for a new way of life, of thinking, building and, in his luggage, quantities of works of art, objects with twenty-two artists, craftsmen and engineers. The new castle was practically finished on his return, so that they only had influence over the finishing touches, except for the gardens, designed and planned by the landscape artist Pacello de Mercogliano. Alas! On the eve of Palm Sunday in 1498 the young King, taking the Queen to see the players of real tennis, in the channels, although very small, hit his head against the lintel of a door to the Hacquelebac gallery, a filthy passage used as a lavoratory. Shortly afterwards he felt ill, lost consciousness and died within nine hours, on a straw mattress in this path, nobody having dared to move him.

Louis XII soon interrupted the works in progress and summoned the masons and architects to Blois, reserving Amboise for Louise of Savoy and her children, François, Count of Angoulême, the future Francis I and Marguerite de Navarre. Francis retained his fondest memory of his adolescence at Amboise where he lived until 1508. Having become king, he took his passion for building elsewhere, not without having completed the wing begun by Louis XII. Under his reign the Court, always on the move, was installed several times at Amboise. It was there on the night of 17 to 18 October 1534, the time of the "placards" affair (Calvinist posters which were aggressively anti-Catholic). The King, sleeping at Blois, found one on the door of his bedroom. It was again at Amboise where Catherine de Médicis took refuge with the Guises, during the plot of March 1560, known as the "Amboise revolt".

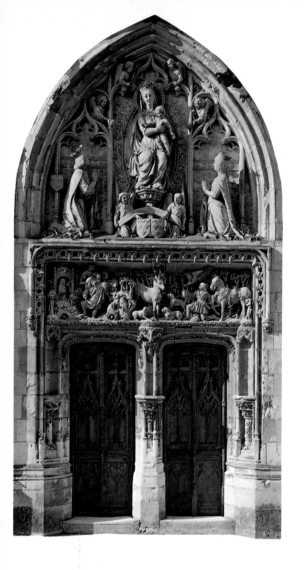

Door of the St-Hubert chapel. The lintel represents the miracle of St-Hubert.

The royal apartments: two views of the guard room.

Condé, a Prince with royal blood and leader of the Huguenot party, aided by La Renaudie, a gentleman from Périgord, intende to seize the young King, Francis II, and murder the Guises. La Renaudie mounted large troops from Brittany by small groups to assemble them and attack the Court where Condé found an excuse to make an appearance. The matter was made known and the royal army surprised the plotters. The repression was atrocious and for a whole day those who had not been hung or quartered had their heads cut off in front of the whole Court, spectators of this expiatory sacrifice.

In the seventeenth century the royal fortress served as a prison for a few important figures such as Fouquet or Lauzun. In the eighteenth century, Louis XV gave it up in favour of Choiseul, raising the fief to a peerage duchy. Louis XVI bought it in 1785 and sold it to the Duke of Penthièvre, father-in-law of the Duke of Chartres, future Philippe Egalité, so that the estate returned to the Orléans after the Revolution. In the meantime the senator Roger-Ducos, to whom Napoleon had entrusted it, demolished all that he could not maintain.

Confiscated after the fall of Louis-Philippe, the castle was the prison of Abd'el Kader and his retinue. The d'Orléans family finally regained possession of the castle which still belongs to it.

Few indications remain as to the buildings prior to the attachment by Charles VII of the seigneury of Amboise to the Crown. Hugues I of Amboise had definitely built, in the first quarter of the twelfth century, a massive fortress, occupying the whole of the natural site formed by the rock platform in the corner of the Loire valley and the valley of the Amasse. The findings and printed plans of J. Androuet du Cerceau, published from 1576 to 1579, show a whole city contained within strong walls. The ambassadors of the sixteenth century wrote that it was more a town than a castle.

In the north, on the Loire, from east to west, the wall falls away abruptly on the rock to which it is bound. Inside rests a gallery of which the skylights can be seen above the curtain wall, flanking as far as the Minimes tower (from the name of the convent of this order, at the foot of the tower), the enchanting gardens which Pacello Mercogliano had designed and planted for Charles VIII.

These gardens were closed off in the south by a gallery and the residences of the canons of the Saint-Florentin collegiate church, which was in the centre of the outer wall. To the west of the Minimes tower is the Charles VIII wing, extended by the curtain wall as far as the round-cornered tower built under Louis XI.

To the east, a straight and rectilinear curtain wall, defended by a moat 20 metres wide, rises at right angles, broken up by the Lions gate, which dates back to the fifteenth century. From the southeastern corner, defended by a bastion and pill-boxes, the curtain wall rejoined towards west-northwest the large Hurtault tower and then the apartment of the Queen, followed by the appartment des Vertus (after the statues representing the seven virtues). The two loggias have disappeared having been

Royal apartments, Charles VIII wing, the state room; below, a Renaissance bedroom.

built for Charles VIII. They were in the late Gothic style, with arched galleries at the ground floor looking out over the courtyard. The walls finally led towards the north-northwest, along a wing now destroyed, which du Cerceau represents as being formed by two superposed wings, very Italian in appearance, and behind which the Saint-Hubert chapel was built. This wing and the wall led to a Louis XI tower, similar to that of the northeast tower, which rejoined in a final section the curtain wall and a block of buildings.

The whole of this vast estate with its outbuildings, its houses, outhouses and church were divided into several courtyards, we might even say several fortresses; one is triangular, the walls and buildings joining together in a triangle at the northwestern corner, closed off at the east by a long main building, with a wide and deep moat on the side of the next courtyard. This second courtyard enclosed the vast space within the Charles VIII wings to the north,

The Louis-Philippe apartments: above, a bedroom; below, the drawing-room.

Right, a detail of the portrait of the King of the French.

over the Loire, the Louis XII and Francis I wings set back, to the east, and the apartments of the Queen and of the seven virtues to the south, separated by a gallery in the east, from the collegiate church.

At the height of the Minimes tower is the accommodation of the royal children. It was at the foot of this building that Charles, having been made King, had the Italian garden laid out.

Several important elements remain of the whole. First of all the outer wall, mostly demolished, and the two large towers: the Minimes one in the centre of the northern wall over the Loire, and the Hurtault one, opposite on the southern wall, looking out over the Amasse. Both date from the time of Charles VIII and have the peculiarity of being enormous towers leading to the castle level by a spiral ramp for horses, even carriages. The Charles VIII wing, with its grated balconies of wrought iron, where the seditious Huguenots were hanged during the Amboise revolt, dominates the Loire, resting on the Minimes tower. On the courtyard side it forms a right angle with the royal apartments built for Louis XII and Francis I.

From the age of Louis XII a gate with a porcupine (emblem of the King),

The Duchess of Mecklemburg-Schweerin, wife of Duke Ferdinand-Philippe d'Orléans, son of Louis-Philippe I, with the young Count of Paris. This Princess "imported" into France the German custom of Christmas trees this painting is nowadays housed in the bishop's palace of the royal chapel of Dreux (Eure-et-Loir).

the remains of a gallery, stands on the terrace where there were once the gardens of Pacello.

The Saint-Hubert chapel, built overhanging the wall, begun in 1491 and ended in 1496, represents, at a time when the King Charles VIII only thought of Naples and Italy, the contribution from Flemish art which was to encounter Italian art in subtle spiritual and technical exchanges.

Above: The dressing room of Charles VIII, known as the Hall of the Drummers (restored in 1995). The king's musicians played here.

Below: Orléans-Penthièvre drawing-room. The Duke of Penthièvre, the maternal grandfather of Louis Philippe, acquired Amboise, which returned to the house of Orléans after the Empire.

Above: The St-Hubert chapel.

Below: The castle with the English park - Oil on canvas by Noël Gustave - 1840.

Ce regard avait 4 siècles d'avance.

LE CLOS-LUCE

The manor of "Cloux", Touraine form of Clos, built in 1477 at the top of Amboise, for Etienne de Loup, a Fleming in the secret services of Louis XI, has all the features of style and construction of the reign: brick and stone anchorages, flamboyant ornaments and a through gallery. The interior, more bourgeois than seigneurial, consists of fine rooms which are fit to live in, the whole surrounded by pleasure and vegetable gardens, orchards and vines.

Charles VIII had bought the residence from his father's servant and it is said that Queen Anne lodged there. Francis I placed it at the disposal of Leonardo da Vinci, when he had convinced the great genius of the sixteenth century to come there, in 1516, to end his days at the Court of France. He died there on 2 May 1519, leaving the three works of art which he had brought with him: the Mona Lisa, Saint Anne and the Virgin and Saint John the Baptist. Leonardo was buried in the cloisters of the Saint-Florentin collegiate church in the heart of the castle. His remains were to be moved into the Saint-Hubert chapel, after the destruction of the collegiate church and a part of the castle under the Empire.

Nowadays Le Clos Lucé holds a museum to the memory of Leonardo da Vinci where the models of some of his inventions are on display.

Above: Leonardo da Vinci, self-portrait in red chalk.

Opposite: the manor on the courtyard side.

Right-hand page: models made by I.B.M. of some of the inventions of da Vinci: the parachute and the wing, inspired by that of bats, the machine gun, the paddle boat and the tank.

Below left: the Mona Lisa (the Louvre).

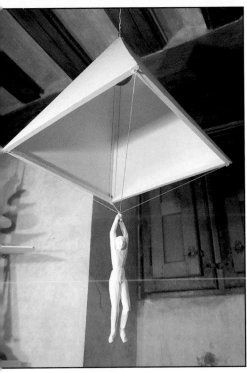

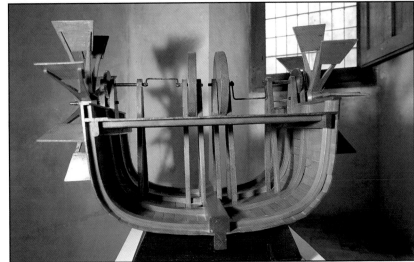

CHISSAY has preserved a large eleventh-century tower. The others date from the sixteenth to seventeenth centuries. The most ancient seigneur known is Robert de l'Isle, in the thirteenth century. In the fifteenth century the land belonged to Bérard, treasurer of Charles VII. It then passed through the hands of several families and had, as the last seigneur, Choiseul, who enlarged his Amboise land. ▲

CHANTELOUP. Choiseul, removed from office, received from Louis XV, in December 1770, the order to retire to Chanteloup. He had built a small Versailles there. Dufort de Cheverny wrote that it was a 20 minutes' walk from his bedroom to that of a friend. It was all demolished in 1823, except for the pagoda, "a sort of a Chinese obelisk", 44 metres high with 7 storeys, built by Le Camus from 1775 to 1776, in homage to loyal friends. ▶

LE GUE-PEAN. Begun by Nicolas Alamand, Angevin financier of Francis I, accused of misappropriation of funds (Beaune Semblançay affair) in 1527, it was continued by his son, François, controller general of the salt taxes then head of the treasury, who died in 1555. The later generations finished building of the estate. ◀

SAINT-AIGNAN-SUR-CHER. The Counts of Blois fortified, in the eleventh century, the rock on the Cher. The castle was transformed at the end of the fifteenth century: the de Husson family, having married into the houses of de La Trémoïlle and de Rohan, rebuilt the main building in brick and stone. Around 1520, Claude de Husson, who was later killed at Pavia, built two wings at right angles in white stone. His daughter, Louise de Beauvilliers, was to complete the work. The Beauvilliers later made a career for themselves at court. Important restoration works, including a "Renaissance style" staircase altered, in the nineteenth century, the harmony of the courtyard. ▶

MONTRICHARD. Around 1020, Hugh I of Amboise built a keep, like in his seigneury of Chaumont. The construction ressembles that of the keep at Loches. The openings and the spiral staircase, housed in a buttress, denote works performed in the second half of the twelfth century. The same period dates the facing of the keep, now demolished, and the curtain wall of the upper terrace. The lower level, from the thirteenth to the fifteenth centuries, was provided with a drawbridge gate, turrets and loggias against the facing of the keep, under Louis XI, who acquired the fief in 1461. ▲

SELLES-SUR-CHER, fortress of the thirteenth century, it belonged to the la Trémoïlle family in the fifteenth century. Charles VII summoned the States General there in 1424 and held counsel before the battle of Orléans in 1429. In 1604 Philippe de Béthune, brother of Sully, bought the land and built, in the enclosure surrounded by moats, a castle with a new design. Two large pavilions remain, linked by a screen wall decorated with regular patterns, opening through a triumphal arch portal; the whole is in brick and tufa. The right-hand pavilion rests on the remains of the former loggia which stretched along the Cher for 34 metres. ▶

CHENONCEAU

In the thirteenth century the seigneur des Marques, vassal of Amboise, held the fief of Chenonceau and that of Houdes, which adjoined it. In 1360 Du Guesclin ousted the English roughnecks who had stayed there despite the treaty of Brétigny. In 1412 Jean I Marques handed his castles over to the English. Charles VII regained them, burnt them and annexed Amboise on which they depended. On 3 April 1432 the King authorised Jean II to rebuild and fortify his castle, which was apparently completed around 1435. Built on the banks of the Cher, on a rectangular masonry base, dropping down to the river in the south and bordered by deep moats on the other sides, it was linked by a bridge to a fortified mill built on two large piers joined by an arch.

In 1460, on the death of Jean II, the inheritance was under threat. Pierre, the oldest of his children, squandered the wealth under the watchful eye of Thomas Bohier from Tours, financier to the Crown, to whom were conferred important duties and functions under three successive reigns.

His father, Austremoine Bohier from the Auvergne, arrived in Touraine with Charles VII, to whom he was secretary, as he was later to Louis XI and Charles VIII, who conferred a title of nobility on him in 1490. He formed an alliance with the du Prat family of financiers from Tours who in the following generation provided an advisor to Francis I. Thomas, who married Katherine Briçonnet, daughter of a superintendent of finances, also from Touraine, and made his career under Charles VIII, Louis XII and Francis I, under whom he was to be treasurer general of the wars in Italy. Dubbed a knight in front of Gênes by Charles d'Amboise, he received the post of lieutenant general of the King in Italy. He died there in 1524.

Such a career had to involve building. Of the sumptuous Bohier hôtel in Tours, only a chimney remains, transferred to the castle

of Plessis-lès-Tours. As for the castellany, Thomas watched over the estate of the Marques family. Patiently he had purchased, in secret, loans and credits on the fiefs and took over the neighbouring estates of Civray, Francueil, La Croix, Bléré, Luzillé, Saint-Georges, Chissay and Chisseau. On 27 April 1496 he gained possession of the seigneury of Houdes, part of the estate, and built a manor there, of which there a few remains today. On 3 June 1496 he forced Marques to sell Chenonceau for 7374 livres and 10 sous (currency of Tours). After proceedings to claim the feudal inheritance, instigated by the heirs, Bohier won his cause in 1512 and became lord of Chenonceau.

Bohier, who had fought a campaign in Italy, returned filled with admiration for the country estates he had seen there, with an open architecture, aimed at pleasing. On their return, kings, important figures, rich bourgeois, more and more joining the nobility, had two choices: fit out and convert the old castle or build a new estate.

Thomas and Katherine Bohier began by choosing the first possibility. In 1513 they summoned masons with experience of the new style from Tours, Amboise and Blois, to update the tower des Marques and the turret joined to it. They had a double stairway built, leading to a terrace and under which opened a descent towards the lower vaulted hall. The frames and the decoration of the entrance door to the turret, with pillars, capitals with mermaids, winged spirits and pediment, fully representative of the new style, were completely inspired by Italy and made by refined decorators, like the pillars flanking the wide mullioned windows, opening towards the Cher, in the two superposed rooms, with fireplaces decorated in the same style. The old keep, crowned by a ceremonial covered way, is decorated by two skylights above the windows and a lantern with conical roofing.

The Bohiers appeared then to want to transform the Marques loggia. They but changed minds, kept the keep and a well, and demolished all the rest. The new castle was built from 1515 to 1522 on the piles of the old fortified mill, at the same time as the Francis I wing was being built at the castle of Blois. Thomas, having left in 1515 for his third Italian expedition, returned there in 1521 with Lautrec, then in 1524, and died there. Therefore Katherine directed the works, employing, it is thought, masons, stonecutters, joiners from Touraine, first-rate craftsmen trained in the late Gothic school, flourishing in the rich merchant and royal town of Tours and highly capable of learning the Italian lesson, which had spread after Charles VIII both in the ornamental style and in the architectural design. The Italians came to Amboise and Blois, and their pupils inevitably influenced the renowned master craftsmen of the Loire valley, linked to one another by strong corporate ties and always willing to learn. Finally the new décor of the des Marques tower, already carried out by others, set the tone.

The plan followed from the base chosen for the castle: the two piles of the demolished mill and the arch which links them form a square base of around 30 metres per side, on which a pavilion was built flanked by corbelled turrets with conical rooves, and extended upstream, to the east, by two avant-corps on the butt of the piers, on the first the chapel and on the second a hall followed by a study.

Each storey has two apartments, separated by a central corridor perpendicular to the river bank, so that one apartment looks out onto the sunrise and the other onto the sunset, each one composed of two main rooms. Between those which look out onto the river downstream, are straight flights of staircase, perpendicular to the axial corridor. This Italian style staircase, composed of two flights separated by a wall, represents a remarkable innovation, at a time when the King was still building at Blois, then at Chambord, perfecting the old model of the spiral of St-Gilles.

The new composition of this castle, born of the restricting arrangement of the building area, avoids the mistake of a massive construction. The lofty turrets, the proportions of the openings, the jutting balconies, the skylights, the projecting parts, contribute to the aesthetic and practical success. The pleasant side of life was not sacrificed, thus the top of the two huge piles which supported the mill was sunk - the one nearest the bank had already been sunk, in part, to house the wheel mechanism - in order to fit, in the northwestern part of the first pile, a room with a semi-circular barrel vault, housing the kitchens. An angled staircase leads down to the Cher under a shelter formed in the southern face of the quay for unloading by delivery boatmen. To the east is a small, less illuminated, room, probably a cellar. A wooden gangway under the arch joins the second quay where the pantry is situated, under two bays of a ribbed vault, with the butchery, smaller, under a barrel vault.

The north and west façades are similar to each other, except for the openings of the central bay. On the north side two pillars decorated like those of the Marques tower frame the entrance supporting the balcony positioned on two bartizan stacks. To the west two large windows illuminate the staircases and the lower opening opens onto a balcony. The two façades are above all decorated by a fine baluster frieze on corbels decorated with leaves and by skylights, some with pilasters, a kiosk in tabernacle flanked by pinnacles, the others with high gables in a triangle, entablature and candelabra, models often imitated, among others, at Chambord. It is probable that the southern face, masked by the gallery built at a later date on the bridge, had the same layout as those of the north and west.

The Bohiers, in order to reach their estates, on the left bank, and their des Houdes manor, travelled by boat. Thomas obtained from the King the letters of patent authorising a bridge over the Cher, a navigable waterway, letters signed at Plessis-lès-Tours in December 1517. The project could not be fulfilled during the lifetime of husband and wife: Katherine, widowed in 1524, died in 1526.

The eldest of their nine children, Antoine, followed in his father's footsteps, and married a daughter of the treasurer general, Poncher, but immediately found himself involved in the operation launched by the King against all financiers and creditors, linked with each other Beaune-Semblançay was hanged at over 80 years old, Antoine's father-in-law was despoiled and hanged ... he himself had to defend his inheritance before the court of accounts and was sentenced to return 90,000 livres to the treasury, and have his property seized. He was forced, in agreement with his brothers and sisters, to sell his castle to Francis I who was to go there in 1538 with Charles V and occasionally to hunt.

Henry II, on his accession, showered his grasping mistress, Diane, with presents and offered her, among other estates, Chenonceau. Since this was property of the Crown, Diane resorted to a subterfuge. The transaction between Francis I and Bohier was cancelled, the latter finding himself once again owner and debtor. Diane bought the land and castle from him on a personal basis, but had nothing to pay, the King having wiped out the debt of Bohier and restored him to his office.

Diane managed the estate like a businesswoman, often staying there, sometimes with Henry II. In 1551 she created, on the right bank, upstream of the castle, gardens and orchards, over two hectares, protected by embankments and surrounded by deep, bricked-up ditches, relying, in order to plant them, on the great owners of the finest gardens and orchards in Touraine.

Philibert Delorme, King's architect, built for Diane the Château d'Anet in 1555. She commissioned from him plans and drawings of the bridge over the Cher, planned by the Bohiers.

Opposite left: fireplace by Jean Goujon, Diane's bedroom.
Above: Louis XIV drawing-room, fireplace with emblems of Francis I and Claude of France.

The works started in 1556. The bridge with five semi-circular arches was ended at the death of the King, but the elegant gallery it was to have borne was not begun. The 9,000 livres of works had been paid by the treasurer of the King's buildings.

A widow, Catherine de Médicis obtained, not without some resistance, the return of Chenonceau to the Crown but gave the former favourite the estate of Chaumont, with its higher income.

The Queen had great plans for Chenonceau. Bullant, her architect, was to make the castle on the Cher the small central pavilion of a grandiose palace. The project was only partly begun. On a vault between the piles, towards upriver, a building joined, on two storeys and an attic, the chapel and library, making the original elegant façade heavy. This addition was eliminated from 1865 to 1875. Also built from 1580 to 1585, was an outer courtyard wing, the current gallery of the domes, three pavilions linked by two low buildings, covered fully by a Delorme framework with domes. These outbuildings were used to house the gentlemen of the household of the Queen Mother, the pantry staff and the chaplain. Catherine then had two storeys of galleries built on the bridge, with a skylighted attic, the whole construction aligned with the west façade seemed much heavier than Delorme had planned. The pavilion which was to end the bridge on the left bank could not be built.

The sojourns of Catherine, despite the civil war, were marked by outstanding celebrations.

Louis XIV by Rigaud.

At the end of March 1560, the Court, after the massacres of Amboise, arrived at the castle for a "triumph" in honour of Francis II and Mary Stuart. The artistic organisation was assigned to the illustrious painter Primatice who had composed décors worthy of antiquity in wich spectacles and celebrations were held until 6 April. They returned in March 1563, after the peace of Amboise, for a kind of dramatic dance of seduction in which the actresses were the daughters of the famous flying squadron of the Queen, disguised as nymphs then as peasant girls, ordered to seduce princes and lords dressed as satyrs or shepherds, all in an extremely permissive atmosphere. The celebrations lasted until 22 April. The climax was however the transvestite orgy offered in 1577 by Catherine to her son, Henry III and the Duke of Anjou. The King and his minions were dressed as women, served by the women of the household of the Queen Mother in very dishevelled men's clothes, their hair in disorder, ready for every indulgence.

Left-hand page, top: bedroom of Gabrielle d'Estrées; bottom: "The Three Graces" by Carl Van Loo (portrait of the three Nesles sisters whom Louis XV intimately honoured). Diane de Poitiers as Diana the Huntress, by Le Primatice.

Above: bedroom of Catherine de Médicis. The Italian-style staircase. Below: the large gallery overlooking the Cher.

Louise de Lorraine, wife of Henry III, learnt at Chenonceau of the murder of the King and prayed, dressed in white - the mourning colour for queens, which she never left off, confined to her furnished apartments decorated with funeral symbols. She lived meagrely, harassed by the creditors of the Queen Mother, ordered to leave before the offer for sale in 1598. Henry IV and his mistress, Gabrielle d'Estrée, having made her bring to reason Philippe of Lorraine, Duke de Mercoeur, her brother and last member of the League, relieved her of her worries for a time, until she died in 1601.

She had donated the castle to César, Duke of Vendôme, legitimate son of Henry IV and of Gabrielle d'Estrée, married to Françoise de Lorraine-Mercoeur, niece of Louise.

Their mother and mother-in-law, the Duchess of Mercoeur, retired to Chenonceau on the death of Henry IV and lived there for 12 years, maintaining the estate and living with great piety, even housing, in the attic, 12 Capucine nuns who were to remain until 1634, 11 years after the death of their benefactress.

In 1733 the Duke of Bourbon Vendôme sold, for 180,000 livres, to Claude Dupin, farmer general, and to his wife, Louise-Marie Madeleine de Fontaine. Dupin, tallage collector at Châteauroux, having obliged the banker Samuel Bernard and his mistress, Madame de Fontaine, was rewarded with the hand of a younger Fontaine and the security of the banker to buy a farm of the ministry of finances. He had a son from a previous marriage who received the Francueil land and took the name of Dupin de Francueil. This son lived with the Dupins.

Chenonceau was then restored to its splendour and furnished and decorated. The Dupins spent every autumn there with their friends and relations from the world of finance but also of literature, arts and sciences, all that the eighteenth century considered intellectual, from Marivaux to Voltaire came to Chenonceau, where Jean-Jacques Rousseau was secretary and tutor to the son of Monsieur and Madame Dupin, a spoilt and difficult child. Child who turned to debauchery and died 1767 as a deportee in the Ile de France (now Mauritius). Dupin died in 1769 at around 88 years old. Madame Dupin, without a direct heir, transferred her affections to the child of Dupin de Francueil, who remarried at the age of 62 with Marie Aurore, the daughter of Maurice de Saxe and of a dancer, widow of the Count de Horn, illegitimate son of Louis XV. From this union was born Maurice François Dupin, future father of Amandine Aurore Lucie Dupin, better known as George Sand, who had memories of her stays at Chenonceau. Madame Dupin ended her days at the castle by leading a quiet and charitable life. She died in 1799, having lived through the Revolution without much trouble; Abbot Lecomte, parish priest, was able to convince the committees that, to suppress the castle, the only link between Montrichard and Bléré, meant going against the interests of the people.

Above: scenes from the waxworks.

Left-hand page, above: bedroom of César de Vendôme - bedroom of the five Queens.
Below: the kitchens.

The last heir of Dupin sold up in 1863 to Madame Pelouze, sister of Daniel Wilson, famous for trading favours. She had the castle renovated as Androuet-du-Cerceau had depicted it.
The estate is nowadays owned by the Menier family who ensure the maintenance of an unbeatable combination: monument, gardens and art collections.

Above: bedroom of the Prince de Talleyrand.

Left-hand page, above: the blue room. Below: bedroom of the King of Spain.

The Princess of Benevento by Madame Vigée-Lebrun.

Villemorien completed the west wing by adding the large south tower, always careful to preserve the unity of Renaissance style, without however avoiding some anachronisms.

He also converted the gallery, doubling the west wing over the courtyard. In 1803 his son sold the estate to Talleyrand, minister of foreign affairs, so that he could have, as Napoleon Bonaparte wished, an estate for receiving foreign diplomats and princes, who were to be praised or seduced. Napoleon made a large contribution to the purchase.

Valençay thus became the castle of the Prince de Talleyrand, "son of a great family, brilliant yet dissolute, dedicated, in spite of himself, to an ecclesiastical career, Bishop of Autun, rejecting the Church to follow the great political transformation whose development he had predicted, a fascinating figure on account of his destiny, his grace, his wit, face, imposing bearing and the disgrace of a club-foot and an amoral soul, dedicated to the cause of the nation through all regimes, serving men as long as they were loyal to his political realism, but nevertheless mercenary and grasping; despicable, admirable, an avid seducer, but still sensitive".

Valençay remained his estate, admirably furnished and decorated, so much that it still seems inhabited by the special genius of an exceptional figure. This estate was also used for the house arrest of the King of Spain Ferdinand VII and his family from 1808 to 1813. Talleyrand, on whom the Emperor imposed this burdensome duty of hospitality, carried out it with much elegance and delicacy which won him the gratitude of the illustrious exiles.

After their departure he regained possession of the castle and restored it to a fit state. Dorothée, wife of his nephew, young and ravishingly beautiful, became the mistress of a household where France and Europe were received.

The diplomat Prince died in Paris in 1838, having finalised a final peace treaty with a minister of the church, who reconciled him, just in time, with God. His body received a Christian burial at Valençay.

Above: the fortified complex of the keep and its walls; in the foreground the towers.

Below: the prison in the new tower.

Insert: dungeon of Lodovico Sforza, Martelet prison.

Right-hand page, top: Cordeliers gate and royal apartments.

Bottom: the royal apartments and the St-Antoine tower.

In the lower chamber of the tower, a wire cage could be suspended for imprisoning important prisoners during the night, to prevent them from escaping. Small in size, it prevented a man of normal height from stretching out completely and moved at the slightest movement, so that it provided great discomfort. Cardinal Balue, guilty of high treason with Bishop Guillaume de Haraucourt, was kept there by Louis XI for a long time. The prelate, bon viveur rather than ascetic, suffered considerably.

The neighbouring Martelet had one storey, not very conspicuous from the courtyard, but with three storeys of dungeons descending into the rock. In the sixteenth century Lodovico Sforza, Duke of Milano, was imprisoned in one of these after having been captured at Novara by Louis XII. He decorated his prison with initials and emblems. Lower down, the bishops of Le Puy and Autun were kept by Francis I, having been involved in the matter of the betrayal of the constable de Bourbon who entered the service of Charles V.

Following the outer wall from the keep towards the northeastern point of the plain, the visitor reaches the collegiate church of Notre-Dame, nowadays the parish church of Saint-Ours, built in the twelfth century by Thomas Pactius, chaplain of the Count of Anjou, Foulques-le-Jeune, with the curious covering of the nave, between the belltowers, by pyramid vaults.

Overlooking the church, protected on all sides by the vertical slope of the rock above the town, itself surrounded by its ramparts, stands the lodging of the King. Built in the fourteenth, fifteenth and sixteenth centuries, it is divided into two parts, the old rooms and the new rooms.

The old rooms date from the end of the fourteenth and beginning of the fifteenth centuries. A tower jutting out over the wall is linked to the old rooms by a narrow passage. Four turrets, covered in stone, divide the façade on the outside, the crenellated covered way, below the sharp slope of the attic, ensures personal defence, the gables are stepped and tall mullioned windows let in plenty of light. The rear façade is framed simply by two turrets. Each level comprises two rooms. In the large ground-floor room Joan of Arc came to remind Charles VII that he had to go to Rheims to be

consecrated. In this part, the same King lived with Agnès Sorel, first official favourite of a French King. She died in 1449 at the age of 28. Her fine marble tomb, after many incidents, was installed in one of the new rooms. The new rooms, added in the extension of the north gable in the fifteenth century by Louis XI, Charles VIII and Louis XII, are built in the style of the late Gothic period with elegant understatement. All military equipment has been removed. On the west façade a loggia with basket-handle arches appears to have been extended by a gallery. The sojourns of Louis XII and Anne of Britanny are marked by the elegant oratory of the Queen, decorated by Breton ermines and Franciscan borders.

LA BOURDAISIÈRE

Situated not far from Montlouis, the fief of La Bourdaisière belonged to Jehan le Meingre, Marshal of Boucicaut, towards the mid-14th century; it then passed to his son, a follower of Du Guesclin and the author of some very interesting memoirs.

In the early 16th century Philibert Babou, born into a family of notaries from Bourges and appointed Finance Minister to King François I, married Marie Gaudin, Lady de la Bourdaisière. He became Mayor of Tours in 1520, and built the Renaissance castle. The beautiful Marie pleasured the King on several occasions. According to chroniclers of the period she frequently engaged in such unarmed combat, as did her three daughters, who enthusiastically served at court. Their son Jean Babou de la Bourdaisière, the first great Knight Commander of Touraine in 1532, married Françoise, daughter of Minister of State Florimont Robertet. They had four sons and six daughters, one of the youngest of whom married Antoine d'Estrées and in 1573 gave birth (apparently at La Bourdaisière) to Gabrielle, who later became the mistress of Henri IV. On Gabrielle's premature death, a Babou cousin consoled the old rake, carrying on the family tradition with a will. Her brother George was killed in a duel, leaving no heir.

Subsequently, the castle was owned by Hercule de Rohan, Duke of Montbazon, Charles d'Albret, Duke of Luynes, and the Duke of Choiseul, exiled to Chanteloup near Amboise, who received it in exchange for land of Cinq-Mars he had bought. He demolished part of La Bourdaisière to deprive his political rival, the Duke of Aiguillon, of the view of it commanded by the latter's Veretz castle. He used the rubble left over from the demolition to build the pagoda of Chanteloup.

Enough remained of La Bourdaisière for the castle to be rebuilt in the 19th century. A casket containing letters from François I to the pretty Babou is said to have been found in a small room; sadly, they were destroyed by the embarrassed daughters of the castle's new owner.

LE PLESSIS-LES-TOURS

The seigneurs of Maillé owned the estate of Les Montils. On 15 February 1463 Louis XI bought it for 5500 gold crowns. The new castle was called "le Plessis du Parc lès Tours". Louis XI made it into a pleasant residence, built of brick and stone. The main wing is formed on the outside by a entresol, two storeys with wide and numerous windows, by an attic with skylights, and over the courtyard by an open gallery, on the ground floor, under the arches from which the openings of the loggia look out, the storey is illuminated by large windows. Three gables, side by side, rise in front of the attic. A chapel extends the wing to the northeast, a staircase tower leads to the storeys in the southwestern corner. Two right-angled wings form the courtyard, with, on the left, a stone façade covered in raised ornaments, lilies, ermines and porcupines, the contribution of Louis XII, with a narrow stairway tower at the gable, then a porch. On the right stand the outbuildings. At the bottom of the courtyard, opposite the central wing, a hedge of bushes stands before the gardens. The right part of the central wing remains, with its staircase tower. Louis XI, an ill man, ended his days at Plessis, protected by all kinds of traps, gratings and pivoting iron turrets while his guard patrolled constantly. Inside, the King lived in well-lit appartments, decorated with paintings, tapestries, surrounded by birds, dogs and exotic animals. Near the castle, a retreat sheltered the holy hermit François de Paule, from Calabria, who died on the estate in 1507.

LUYNES

LUYNES, bearing the name of Maillé until 1619, stands on the right bank of the Loire. The first keep, demolished by Foulques le Réchin, Count of Anjou, in 1096 and rebuilt in the following 10 years by Hardouin de Maillé, played an important role in the war of the Counts of Anjou against those of Blois, in that of the Capetians against the Plantagenets and in the Hundred Years' War.

Built under the reign of Saint Louis, the castle forms a square, with four round corner towers and four round towers in the middle of the curtain wall, ensuring crossed flanking, without dead angles. The ancient descriptions of the thirteenth and sixteenth centuries mention a powerful central keep. There is nothing left of it. The north and east faces are separated from the plain by a wide dry ditch. The entrance opens near the northeast tower which covered it. The drawbridge was replaced by a fixed bridge in the nineteenth century.

After having sold les Montils to Louis XI to build le Plessis there, Hardouin de Maillé invested his 5500 gold crowns in building, against the west wall of his castle, a replica of the new royal castle, the same bond of brick and stone, the same fine and light windows, the same staircase tower, so that Luynes gave a more complete image of Le Plessis than Le Plessis itself.

The south part of the loggia was rebuilt at the end of the sixteenth century or the beginning of the seventeenth, then restored in the nineteenth and twentieth centuries, as was the whole of the castle.

The seigneury of Maillé, which in 1501 passed to the house of Laval, had been sold in 1619 to Charles d'Albert, lord of Luynes, from the name of a small area in Provence. This gentleman was well-versed in the art of hawking. Chosen as the great falconer of the young Louis XIII, he gained his friendship and helped him to remove Concini and his wife, Italian adventurers who had won over the Queen Mother, Marie de Médicis. Luynes obtained permission from the King to give the name of Luynes to the land of Maillé, raised to a peerage duchy. He remained in grace for slightly less than five years then the King saw that the man no longer deserved his friendship.

VILLANDRY

Secretary of State at the Treasury under Francis I, Jean Breton, captured at Pavia with the King, and returning from captivity in 1527, had begun building his castle of Villesavin, near Chambord, when he purchased, in 1532, the seigneury of Villandry, looking out over the Cher, in this valley which this river, running to it, shares with the Loire.

It was a feudal castle bearing the name of Colombiers. Henry II Plantagenet had come there in 1189 to ask for peace with Philip Augustus, before surrendering at Azay, and then taking refuge at Chinon, to die there on 6 July 1190. The keep, redesigned in the fourteenth century, was preserved by Jean Breton and included in the new castle which he then undertook to build.

Apart from this keep, he retained the base surrounded by moats with water from the old feudal castle and built, in one piece (the site closed in 1536), the last great Renaissance castle in the Loire valley. It is still possible to make out the influence of Chambord or of Blois, but the models are instead the Fontainebleau of the courtyard of La Fontaine and of the "Porte Dorée" gate, and Ecouen, which were being built at that time.

Opposite right: the keep of Villandry.

The third Renaissance garden combines simple herb, aromatic and medicinal plants on a higher level, a water garden surrounded by a cloister of vegetation in the style of the reign of Louis XV, completes this museum of gardens.

One needs to walk in the privileged area of the gardens at Villandry to understand the role given to the estate near the castle, made to be seen from the windows, to complete the living space, stretching the décor offered to the guests as far as the woods and fields, in the spirit of a true art of living.

Above, the large drawing-room (18th century).

Below, the green room (18th century).

Above: the dining-room (18th century)
Below: "Bread", school of the painter Zurbaran (17th century Spain).
Opposite: "The Philosopher in the Mirror" by the painter Schönfeld (1609-1682) illustrates Socrates' theme, "Know thyself."

The gardens. Above, the gardens of love; below, on both sides of the canal, the gardens of "pleasure," replicas and continuation of the castle reception rooms.

AZAY-LE-RIDEAU

Built on an island encompassing the Indre between 1518 and 1527, Azay, like Chenonceau, is the work of one of the most wealthy financiers of Tours, Gilles Berthelot, master of accounts, treasurer of France and mayor of Tours.

His father, Martin Berthelot, master of public monies of Louis XI then of Charles VIII, had bought the seigneury towards the end of the fifteenth century. It was a very old fief, belonging in the twelfth century to Master Ridel, who gave it his name. A fortified keep controlling the ford of the Indre probably stood on the site of the tower of the present castle.

In 1418, Charles, dauphin, for one year escaped the Anglo-Burgundians, who had seized, by treachery, Paris and the King, Charles VI. Having taken refuge at Bourges, he controlled Berry, Orléanais and Touraine and rode ceaselessly, with his army, around his tragically depleted kingdom. Passing through Azay, he found the fortress, with the captain and 350 soldiers (a number which indicates the importance of the fortress), rallied with the Burgundians, insulting him from the covered way. The future Charles VII stopped his standards, laid siege to the keep and captured it: the whole garrison was hanged, village and castle burnt. The example has remained in people's memories: one hundred years later it is still referred to as "Azay-le-Brûlé".

The staircase and its loggias in the Italian style.

Gilles Berthelot, having inherited in 1518, immediately undertook construction of a new castle, with the aid of his wife, Philippe Lesbahy. His responsibilities kept Gilles away too often, so Philippe, as Katherine Briçonnet had done at Chenonceau under the same circumstances, supervised the works and had to make a number of decisions, justifying the often expressed impression of a feminine work. She nevertheless benefitted from the advice of Guillaume Artault, priest of Saint-Cyr.

The L-shaped plan was not as such an original feature, nor a whim, but evidence that the castle could not be finished, in spite of the activity of Lady Berthelot and by the master masons: Denis Guillourd who prepared

The flat vaults of one of the flights of the staircase. Each bay contains two portraits, with a finely chiselled profile, of kings or queens facing each other. The bays rest on arches springing on matching keystones, elaborately decorated.

he foundations on piles, then Etienne Rousseau leading sixteen workmates ... In 1517 in fact Francis I, seeking someone to blame for the defeat at Pavia and to provide the huge ransom set by Charles V, took it out on the war treasurers, the financiers, his creditors whom he had had judged, despoiled and even hanged like Semblançay. All of them, or nearly all, were from Touraine and connected by a network of marriages and family alliances.

Gilles Berthelot was cousin of the great minister of finance Semblançay, taking sides with him, like Bohier de Chenonceau, Poncher and Hurault de Cheverny, in the financial deals, the accounts expedients, in which all these financiers had to engage to maintain their fortunes in such a healthy condition that they could always respond to royal demands. Gilles Berthelot fled to Metz in Lorraine and died in Cambrai in 1529. The castle, seized in 1528, was given by the King to Antoine Raffin, his companion at arms at Marignano and Pavia and later his ambassador in several kingdoms. Such as it is, the castle offers a prime example of the art of the early Renaissance, so typical of the Loire valley. Like at Blois and Chambord, the façades are divided into regular surfaces by the square patterns of the mouldings and bands marking the horizontal levels and by the pillars punctuating the bays, from the dado to the pedimented skylights.

Here however the massive corner towers of Chambord are transformed into elegant suspended turrets and the staircase of Blois, spiral of Saint-Gilles, added onto the façade, makes way for, like at Chenonceau, an admirable staircase in the Italian style, with straight flights, on three storeys of loggias of which the semi-circular openings, projecting half a storey in relation to those of the bays of the façade, distinguish this building, detached like a major ornamental theme, but still in harmony with the whole of the façade into which it is integrated. The emblems on the balustrades of the loggias, the initials on the pediments, of Francis I and Claude of France, who died in 1524, date this

Above, the Biencourt drawing-room in the great hall on the ground floor, the Renaissance-style fireplace with salamander, restructured in the 19th century in the style of Fontainebleau.
Below: the kitchens.

Blue room: above, four-poster bed with embroidered canopy (late 18th century) and Lille tapestry (late 17th century), "royal houses" series; on the decorative panel of the fireplace, Louis XIV, (Mignard school); below, duck-hunting scene, Beauvais tapestry (1705).

Right, royal bedroom - Louis XIV slept here - left, 17th century bed and Paris tapestry, first half of the 17th century, cartoon by Simon Vouet, scene from the romance Rinaldo and Armide, inspired by Torquato Tasso's Jerusalem delivered; to the right, early 17th century cabinet, burnished pear-wood decorated with slabs engraved after Jacques Callot and tapestry from the same Rinaldo and Armide series.

Opposite: "The Field of Cloth of Gold" (1520) by Boutewerk (copy of the original found in London). It shows various scenes from the meeting between Francis I and Henry VIII.

architectural treasure. Unfortunately the salamanders, the ermines and initials to be found too in the patterns of the interior décor, homages to the sovereigns, were not to save the Berthelots from disgrace.

The west wing, which joined the former keep, replaced in the nineteenth century by the large round tower, was to have been balanced by a symmetrical wing to the east, framing the main courtyard. Since there was no wing, a turret was added to the corner of the central building, on the courtyard. This is the sole addition, with the large tower, to the work of art built in nine years, by Gilles and his wife Philippe. The delicate crown of the ornamental covered way reminds us of the ambition of these new seigneurs from Touraine, often disappointed in their luck.

Servants and courtisans of luck, the Berthelots knew its fatal versatility, builders of the most exquisite estate, they never lived there.

Many families came to Azay, the last one, that of the Marquis and Marquess de Biencourt, stayed there for four generations, from 1787 to 1899 and took care of maintenance and restoration of the castle. The de Biencourt family survived the Revolution without any crises, executions or demolitions, demonstrating considerable broad-mindedness.

It was during the time of the Marquis Antoine-Marie de Biencourt, that Balzac, a guest at the very close castle of Saché, wrote "The Lily in the Valley", of which a part of the setting is directly inspired by the valley of the Indre and its fine estates. He often came to Azay whose grace he loved, comparing the castle with a diamond set in the landscape of the park and river banks. Requisitioned by the Prussians in 1871, this gem was nearly burnt by Prince Frédéric-Charles of Prussia. The accidental fall of a central light in the kitchens where he was dining made him think he was the victim of an attack. His officers fortunately brought him to his senses.

The government, purchaser of the castle in 1905, ensures its upkeep and restoration and opens to the public furnished apartments and in particular a fine collection of Flemish tapestries of the sixteenth and seventeenth centuries.

SACHÉ

Saché Castle, once a baron's seat, situated on the left bank of the Indre upstream of Azay-le-Rideau, had large domains consisting of fields, vineyards and woods. It belonged in turn to various families of the Tours bourgeoisie. The presence of the King as from the 15th century increased their prosperity, based on administrative and financial appointments and trade, and they often gained entry to the minor nobility.

The Lord of Saché built his Renaissance castle in the 16th century. In the late 18th century it belonged to the Savary family, whose daughter Anne married her cousin, Jean de Margonne, bringing the castle and lands of Saché, with three manors, farms and windmills, as her dowry. The castle was then partly converted.

Jean de Margonne was a close friend of Bernard-François Balzac, the son of a Tarn farmer called Balssa. Balzac had studied as a clerk in notaries' offices in his province, and later in Paris. He rose by degrees in his profession, manifesting such intelligence and energy that he became secretary to the Council of State and administrator of the armed services during the revolution. He eventually came to Tours as administrator of the funds destined for the Vendée army.

In 1797 he was still in Tours, in charge of supplies, well-off but not rich. At the age of 51 he married nineteen-year-old Laure Salembier, the pretty, coquettish, hard-hearted daughter of rich Parisian drapers. Their son Honoré was born in Tours in 1799 (a first child having died in infancy in 1798), followed by his sister Laure in 1800, another sister, Laurence, in 1802, and a younger brother Henry in 1807.

Henry, whom his mother unkindly preferred to Honoré, was probably the issue of the affair between the ever-charming Madame Balzac and M. de Margonne, the owner of Saché Castle, yet the situation did not cause any rift between the two families. Bernard-François Balzac, who was 32 years older than his wife and obsessed with longevity, is said to have had no objection to proxies. As for M. de Margonne, his wife was good and virtuous but morose and deformed.

In any event, the Margonne household always showed great affection for Honoré (de) Balzac. With them, especially between 1829 and 1837, he found unreserved hospitality, a refuge from his creditors, models for his characters in the local society, and the landscapes and scenarios of novels set in Tours, right down to the composition of the bouquets of wild flowers made by Félix de Vandenesse for Henriette de Mortsauf in *Le lys dans la vallée*.

In his room at Saché Balzac wrote *Le Père Goriot, Maître Cornélius* and *Louis Lambert*. *César Birotteau* was created there, in a single sitting. Numerous letters were sent from or to Saché by the author. This room, its furniture and the setting of the home where Balzac lived are preserved or reconstructed in a very attractive, evocative Balzac Museum; as well as the objects used by the writer, it contains numerous manuscripts, editions and a major iconography. Admirers of Balzac should definitely make the pilgrimage to Saché.

LANGEAIS

There are two castles at Langeais which mark the beginning and end of military constructions in the Middle Ages. The first, fortress of Foulques Nerra, dates from the end of the tenth or the beginning of the eleventh century. At the end of the present park stand important remains corresponding to the narrowing of the promontory: the bases of an advanced tower, then those of the ancient castral chapel. Forty steps backwards, the base of a small-bonded ashlar wall forms a right angle and bars the spur, in front of a deep moat before the keep, of which the openings, at 3 metres from the former ground, and the thickness of the walls rapidly reduced to 0.70 m, suggest that this was not a proper keep but instead a castral estate, later reinforced and converted into a fortress during the wars between the Counts of Anjou and those of Blois, then between the Kings of England and those of France. In 1189 the victory of Philip Augustus over Henry II of England transformed the political landscape of the Loire valley. From 1206 onwards Langeais was a royal fortress.

In the thirteenth century Pierre de la Brosse, from Touraine, at the service of Saint-Louis as a barber-surgeon, struck a friendship with the dauphin Philip. Philip and Pierre de la Brosse were in Tunis when the King died from the plague in 1270. Philip III made Pierre his chamberlain. The favourite received Langeais with many other seigneuries, and then suffered various fates, made jealous enemies, was accused of plotting and, having fallen into disgrace, was hanged in 1278. From then Langeais does not figure in history and chronicles until

the arrival in Touraine of Charles VII. This fortress on the right bank could be dangerous if the English were to stay there. Charles bought the seigneury and demolished the fortifications, apart from the large tower.

The name of Langeais reappeared under Louis XI with Jean Bourré, born in Angers in 1424, son of a bourgeois from Château-Gonthier. This lawyer entered the service of the dauphin Louis, who opposed his father Charles VII, and followed him to Dauphinois as secretary and right-hand man, both his chancellor and accountant. When Louis XI came to power, Jean retained the same privileges and functions, but at the level of the kingdom and became a great figure. At the time of the war of the public good (revolt by the princes and great feudal lords against the royal power which Louis was patiently trying to consolidate) Jean Bourré, in charge of financing and control of the works of the royal fortresses in Touraine, was appointed captain of Langeais. Francis II, Duke of Brittany, was a member of the League and represented a threat on the northwestern front of Touraine. Jean Bourré decided to rebuild Langeais which enclosed the Loire upstream of Tours and the Brittany road. The new fortress, facing towards the village and the Loire, was built at the end of the promontory. The buildings were paid for by Jean Briçonnet, treasurer and mayor of Tours from 1465 to 1467.

The construction model adopted is that of the great fortresses of the fifteenth century, like Pierrefonds. Some technical peculiarities can be

Opposite left: the castle of Foulques-Nerra.
Above: the marriage hall.
Below: the courtyard "La Chapelle"
Left-hand page: diptych of Charles VIII and Anne of Brittany.

noted, such as the false breeches at the foot of the towers and of the curtain walls, terraces allowing grazing fire and the upper storey of the towers, set back, covering the covered way. The works proceeded at a fast rate: a lodgings in two blocks and two open-angle round towers, and finally the entrance, its drawbridge and the large tower at the end. The fortified complex was protected by moats, supplied with water by the Roumer, and partially filled in. The works were then stopped, the courtyard, whose façade is ornamented by numerous wide openings and three spiral staircase towers, an annexe, was never closed off by towers or curtain walls. The war of the public good ended in 1465, the Duke of Brittany was defeated in Normandy, peace was returned to the Loire and Langeais lost its strategic importance. Jean Bourré, discharged from Langeais, was able to dedicate himself to building a "modern" castle on his land at Plessis-Bourré.

In 1466, Louis XI gave Langeais to François d'Orléans, Count of Longueville and of Dunois, son of the famous bastard of Orléans. He completed the castle by the building of adjacent loggias including that of the guard room, on the ground floor and the large hall upstairs.

Dunois was the instigator of the breaking of the marriage engagement between Margaret of Burgundy, daughter of Maximilian, future emperor of Austria and Charles VIII, and that between Anne of Brittany and the same Maximilian. The aim was to unite Charles VIII and Anne of Brittany and to link indissolubly the kingdom and the duchy of Brittany. After having organised the separation of Charles and Margaret at Baugé, Dunois, on leaving the town fell from his horse and was killed on 25 November 1491. On 6 December 1491, in his castle of Langeais, the marriage was held between Charles VIII and the Duchess Anne, which was to settle definitively the question of the Brittany succession.

Langeais belonged to several families then to the Duke of Luynes. His son managed to keep Langeais, and his head, during the Revolution. The castle then finally passed to the Moisant family, bourgeois from Tours, then Baron, solicitor from Paris and collector, whose son squandered

his assets. Jacques Siegfried bought the property in 1885 and spent, with the aid of his wife, twenty years of his life in restoring the castle with skill, in furnishing it and enriching the collections of furniture, objets d'art, works of art and above all of tapestries, to reform, within the virtually intact setting of this monument, the interior of a great seigneur or of a great prince at the end of the fifteenth century.

The Institut de France, legatee of Jacques Siegfried, ensures the preservation of his work.

Above: tapestry of the crucifixion (end of the sixteenth century). Below: panel of the dawn (around 1530) - the shrine, painted and gilded wood (end of the thirteenth century). Right-hand page, top: bedroom of the aristolochia (tapestry of the second half of the sixteenth century). Below: the guard room.

USSÉ

The known history of this fief begins in the fifteenth century with the building by the Bueil family, on the site of an ancient fortress, of a castle very close in its technical design to that of Langeais.

Jean de Bueil, one of the main captains of Charles VII, had already rebuilt Montrésor. He died in 1477. His son Antoine, who had married one of the daughters of the King and of Agnès Sorel, sold the castellany to Jacques d'Espinay in 1485. This lord, who had been chamberlain of Louis XI and of Charles VIII, succeeded by his son Antoine, built the west wing and formed an entrance, protected by two towers, in the east wing. Jacques d'Espinay had, in his will, decided on the building of a collegiate chapel to the east of the castle. Charles, his son, and Lucrèce de Pons, his daughter-in-law, carried out his wishes from 1523 to 1535. It was consecrated in 1538 under their son, René, who signed the foundation of the college of the canons assigned to perform services.

Charles and Lucrèce d'Espinay also created the Renaissance façade and the west wing of the inner courtyard.

In 1659 the land was bought by the marquis Bernin de Valentinay. In order to open out the three wings of the castle onto the valley, he had the north wing eliminated, as the owner of Chaumont will do later, and built for his son, who married the daughter of the Marshal de Vauban, a classical wing with three pavilions, on the other side of the northwest tower, as if he had wanted to displace laterally the volume of the demolished north wing. The marquis de Valentinay was responsible for the terraces of the gardens which descended towards the river Indre, terraces which in the summer are brightened by orange trees in tubs, several of which were planted under the Ancien Régime.

The castle later belonged to the Duke of Montbazon, Monsieur de Chalabre, the Duchess de Duras and the Countess de la Rochejacquelin, who passed it on to her nephew, Count de Blacas, whose descendants still own Ussé.

All the buildings of the fifteenth century formed a closed-off rectangle, flanked by high, round towers, resting, at the south, on the slope where the massif of the vast forest of Chinon ended. The north wing, no longer there, formed the main block, opposite and parallel to the Indre, while the south wing originally was only a simple curtain wall linking the east and west wings and extending as far as the keep, built outside of the outer wall, in the southwestern corner.

The affinities with Langeais are numerous: above all the continuous covered way, the upper storey of the towers, set back from this covered way and allowing it to be kept, beneath firing, the entrance between two towers, in the northeastern corner of the quadrilateral, which was condemned in the seventeenth century.

The difference in the levels of the covered way of the style of the machicolation enable several stages of building to be detected. The north wing, no longer there, but whose origins remain, the south wing, the keep, the south half of the east wing, are allegedly the work of Jean V de Bueil, and later of his son Antoine. This wing was completed, at the end of the fifteenth century and at the beginning of the sixteenth, by Jacques d'Espinay and by Antoine d'Espinay, his son.

As for the three façades over the courtyard, they have been rebuilt in different periods. That of the east wing, very plain originally and intact in the nineteenth century, was then heavily restored in the Gothic style and the south façade was redesigned according to tastes of the seventeenth century, and opened by large, very classical windows. As for the façade of the west wing, it was rebuilt in the sixteenth century in a Renaissance style similar to that of the Francis I wing of the castle of Blois.

The collegiate church to the east of the castle, in the park, marks the passage from Gothic to Renaissance, built from 1523 to 1535 by Charles d'Espinay and Lucrèce de Pons, whose initials C and L appear in the ornaments, outside and inside the building. Its structure is very Gothic, composed of four rib-vaulted bays, while the ornamentation, in particular that of the entrance portal, with its pillars, medallions, tympanum shell and ornaments of the bands, mark the Italianising trend, later and more discreet, in religious monuments in France.

Ussé, in its leafy setting, topped with several towers and pinnacles, surrounded by such a rich machicolation, has attracted Charles Perrault, travelling in Touraine, in wich he his supposed to have recognised the real castle of the Sleeping Beauty, the first of his fairy tales, published in the "Mercure Galant" of 1696. He may have arrived, through the forest of Chinon, to the house of the Bernin de Valentinay family, one day when everybody was still asleep...

In actual fact, everything in the castle is set out for the visitor to find again, as if by magic, in the salons, the galleries or the bedroom of the King, lords and ladies dressed in the finest costumes of their times and about to come to life, like in the fairy tale.

Left-hand page, from left to right: the east wing on the courtyard side, the west wing, the castle of seventeenth century, in the middle distance, the keep. In the foreground, the terrace and its orange trees.

Below: the east façade.

Apse of the collegiate church. *Overall view from the south east.*

The inner façade of the east wing.

Above right: the bedroom of the king; below: the old guard room.

Florentine secrétaire (16th century).

Téniers gallery, series of Flemish tapestries on Téniers cartoons (17th century).

Once upon a time… Sleeping Beauty: the king and the queen, the fairy, Beauty and the old woman at the spinning wheel, Beauty's reawakening.

CHINON

The position of the Chinon rock has always been a strategic site. The Roman and Gallo-Roman camp, of which elements of masonry are to be found in the foundations of the castle, made way for a Gallic fortress, with several prehistoric settlements in the meantime.

In the south, the cliff drops sharply to the bed of the Vienne, and in the west and to the north, a short but deep limestone gorge isolates the rock. To the east a slight undulation separates it from the coast which continues and, on this side, the defences were reinforced. The towers and watch dominate the valleys of the Vienne and Loire, as far as Saumur, Sainte-Maure, l'Ile-Bouchard....

The oldest mention of Chinon is to be found in Grégoire de Tours, who tells of the siege of 446 by Aegidius, Roman governor of Gaul. The town was at that time Visigothic.

History recalls it in the tenth century. Chinon belonged at that time to the Counts of Blois who were fighting against the Counts of Anjou. After the battle of Saint-Martin-le-Beau, Thibault III of Blois gave up Chinon, Tours and Langeais to Geoffroy Martel, Count of Anjou, known as Plantagenet and husband of Matilda, heiress to the crown of England. Her son, Henry, enclosed it. He made Chinon the heart of his French possession. This led to the conflict between the King of France and his vassal, the King of England.

Henry II Plantagenet completed the general layout of the fortifications by large buildings, including the St-Georges fort. Towers and curtain walls were reinforced and modernised. He died at Chinon after the treaty of Azay in 1189.

His son Richard the Lionheart, wounded at Chalus, came back and died in Chinon. His brother John Lackland succeeded him.

In 1202 Philip Augustus began the reconquest, took Château-Gaillard in Normandy, attacked Chinon in 1204, lifted the siege in winter, took Loches after Easter of 1205 and Chinon for Midsummer's Day. Touraine was once again French. He renewed the fortifications and re-armed the fortress which he had left in a sorry state. He himself, Louis IX, and Philippe III often stayed there.

The fortress played an important role in the campaigns against the English and against the rebelling vassals. In 1308, en route for Poitiers, where Pope Clement V intended to interrogate them, the dignataries of the order of Templars, including the great master, Jacques de Molay, were imprisoned, by order of Philip the Fair, in a tower of the castle. The following year, having been transferred to Paris, they were burnt alive.

From 1425 the dauphin, the future Charles VII, made Chinon his capital in the heart of the martyred kingdom.

In early 1429 Joan of Arc arrived at the castle and in the evening of 9 March she entered the great hall of the royal apartments and marched confidently towards the dauphin, even though he deliberately mingled with his gentlemen, officers and advisors

Above, from left to right (from west to east): the Coudray fort, the Milieu fort, the Clock tower, beyond this tower, the St-Georges tower.
Opposite: the Clock tower.

and was less richly dressed than them. Although modest, she was just as comfortable as if she already frequented the Court. Charles pretended, for a joke, not to be the dauphin, but Joan was not to be waylaid and told him, to confirm her mission, a secret, which only he could know. Thus he was immediately convinced, in spite of the hesitancy of his retinue, always worried about sharing influence over the Prince. Thus the reconquest started from Chinon.

Around 1442, Charles met Agnès Sorel, fell in love with her, and made her one of the ladies-in-waiting of the Queen and lodged her in a private mansion, Roberdeau, in front of the north wall of the castle, which he was able to reach via an underground passage.

Louis XI, Charles VIII and Louis XII were several times at Chinon, the latter receiving there, on 18 December 1498, Cesare Borgia, emissary of the pope, his father. He bore the bull of annulment of the marriage of Louis and Jeanne of France, allowing the King to marry Anne of Brittany.

After varying fortunes, Chinon came under the supervision of Richelieu and his heirs who left the castle to fall into ruins.

The outer wall forms an extended quadrilateral around four hundred metres long by seventy metres wide, and follows closely the shape of the rocky spur. It is divided into three fortresses separated by deep moats, that is to say from east to west, the Saint-Georges fort, the castle of Milieu, the fort of Coudray. Of the Saint-Georges fort, built by Henry II Plantagenet, only a crypt, that of the St-Georges chapel, remains. The second fortress, known as the "fort du Milieu", is flanked by more widely spaced towers, this disadvantage remedied by

Above: St Martin, polychrome wood (16th century). Royal apartments, room where Joan of Arc was received (opposite), and the kitchens (below); on the walls, Aubusson tapestry (17th century): Joan of Arc recognizes the Dauphin at Chinon.

reflex angles in the line of the curtain walls. Entrance is through the clock tower. It is there where the royal lodgings stood under Charles VII. The west wall and the fireplace of the great throne room where Joan of Arc was received can still be seen. The other rooms have been made into a museum. Finally the fort of Coudray, built on a very sophisticated polygonal plan, avoids any dead angles, with closely positioned towers flanking the curtain walls. Barbicans, facings and counterscarp walls were added to the defences of the forts as well as the walls and defences of the town.

Rabelais (gallery of the castle of Beauregard)

LA DEVINIERE, François Rabelais, born in Chinon (1494-1533), rue de la Lamproie, son of a lawyer, has been a monk, doctor, hellenist and the author, in five volumes, of the lives of Gargantua and of his son Pantagruel. He often lived, in his childhood, at la Devinière, his father's country house, and took the whole small region of Chinon as his setting for the narration of the pichrocholine war (Gargantua, 1st volume). ▲

LE RIVEAU. Pierre de Beauvau, chamberlain of Charles VII, obtained permission from the King, in 1442, to restore the thirteenth-century castle which his wife had provided as a dowry. He kept the square plan and, probably, that of the massive keep. A staircase turret leads to the covered way. Round towers flank the curtain wall at the corners; a staircase tower leads to the accommodation. The façade which closes off the courtyard and its chapel were destroyed in the eighteenth and nineteenth centuries. Le Riveau is given by Gargantua, at the end of the pichrocholine war, to Tolmère, like Montsoreau to Ithybole (Rabelais, "Gargantua", Chapter 51). ▼

MONTSOREAU, rebuilt in the middle of the fifteenth century by Jean de Chambes, advisor to Charles VII, looks out over the Loire which, until 1820, washed against the high wall. The building forms a wide rectangular keep which is completed by two wings. Charles de Chambes made his name in an unfortunate manner under Charles IX as executioner of Saint-Barthélémy in Anjou. The same lord had married the beautiful Françoise de Méridor. This lady made a rendezvous with Bussy d'Amboise, who had boasted of seducing her, at the castle of Coutancière, in collusion with her husband. Bussy, awaited by the people of Chambes, was murdered; this was in 1579. The lord and lady lived then for many years and had nine children .... Alexandre Dumas wrote a novel, not a very historical one, based on their story - "La Dame de Montsoreau". ▼

MONTREUIL-BELLAY. The outer wall surrounding the escarpment which looks over le Thouet, a curtain wall flanked by large round towers and watchtowers, protects several buildings: the old castle, the new castle and the collegiate church. Originally there was a fortress of Foulques Nerra, contested, demolished, rebuilt and finally conquered by Philip Augustus. In the fifteenth century, Guillaume d'Harcourt, without claiming to compose an architectural whole, took measures to build, reinforce or reconstruct, from 1428 to 1484, the outer wall and the different buildings with the aim of military efficiency. In the middle of the courtyard, he kept the ancient keep, destroyed in the nineteenth century. At the entrance, on the town side, he integrated the thirteenth-century fort in a vast defensive building. Slightly further on, he erected a collegiate chapel, consecrated in 1484. In the west corner of the outer wall he restored the "miniature castle" to house the chaplains of the collegiate chapel. The kitchen with a central chimney is based on that of Fontevraud. Finally, to the north, on the escarpment above le Thouet, stands the new castle, adapted technically to the new forms of warfare, without machicolation but with terraced towers to manoeuvre artillery weapons. As for lodgings, they show an attempt at comfort and luxury.

FONTEVRAUD

The kitchens.

Robert d'Arbrissel, born around 1047 near Rennes, priest and theologian, later travelling preacher, had a large number of disciples, penitents and convertees. He settled his flock in the forest of Fontevraud in 1099, founding an original monastery consisting of four separate communities: le Grand Moûtier for the nuns, Ste-Madeleine for the penitent girls, St-Lazare for the lepers and St-Jean for the monks, chaplains and those in charge of secular matters. An abbess governed the whole complex, always chosen from princely families or those of high nobility. Her power extended to all the possessions of the order. Building of the monastery began in 1101, funded by the Counts of Anjou, who chose to rest there, and by their vassals. It was to be restarted and continued up until the seventeenth century.

The abbey-church, the famous Roman kitchen, the chapter house, the St-Benoît infirmaries and the St-Lazare priory remain of the monastic town.

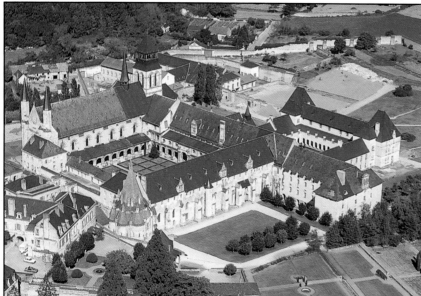

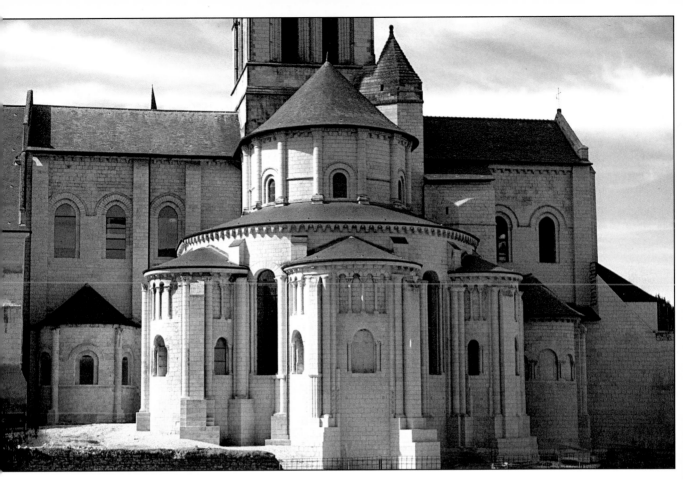

Fontevraud abbey (12th century). Above, the choir with apse with three absidioles and the transept. Each wing has a chapel facing east.

Below, the nave and the cupola vaults; the choir at the end.

Fontevraud abbey (12th century). Above, reclining polychrome tufa figures (early 13th century) of Eleanor of Aquitaine, queen of France and then queen of England, buried in 1204, and Henry II Plantagenet, king of England, her husband, buried in 1189. Below: reclining polychrome wood figure (mid-13th century) of Isabella of Angoulême, buried in 1246, second wife of John Lackland, king of England, and reclining polychrome tufa figure (early 13th century) of Richard the Lion-Hearted, king of England, buried in 1199. Richard and John were the sons of Henry II and Eleanor.

SAUMUR

The keep of Saumur was taken from the Count of Blois, Thibault le Tricheur, by the Count of Anjou, Foulques Nerra. Geoffrey Plantagenet rebuilt the fortress. In 1203 Philip Augustus definitively annexed it to the kingdom. His grandson, Louis IX, built, on the original site, a new fortress from 1227 to 1230 and gave it as a privilege in 1246 to his brother, Charles d'Anjou.

This castle was composed of four irregular sides, flanked by round corner towers. The foundations are still visible at the foot of the north and west towers, and the original vaults can be found on the inside.

In 1360 the younger son of Jean Le Bon, Louis, received Anjou as a privilege. He was the brother of Charles V, who renovated the Louvre, of the Duke of Berry, and of the Duke of Burgundy, all keen on art, architecture and chivalry. The Duke chose Saumur to rebuild his finest castle there. On the basis of the castle of Saint-Louis, an austere fortress, he built this extraordinary synthesis of fortress and enchanted palace, of which "Les Très Riches Heures" of the Duke of Berry, kept in the Condé museum at Chantilly, has conserved the picture, painted by Jean Colombe (1480). The comparison of the present castle with the miniature proves the accuracy, although a number of elements have disappeared including the top and the ornaments of the towers. There is further confirmation also in the minute details of the accounts kept by Macé Darne, master of the works, which have been handed down to us for a part of the works campaign, from 1367 to 1376, the date of his death. The northwest wing of which this first master of the works makes no mention, and was thus built after his death, was eliminated at the end of the seventeenth century. The corner towers which frame it have remained.

Joining the north tower to the gallery of the east wing, the main staircase opens, over the courtyard, its four storeys of ceremonial balconies,

where we can picture the Prince and the court watching a spectacle or the entry of important persons. The niches, on either side of the loggias, contained statues of the Duke of Anjou, of his brothers, King Charles V, the Dukes of Berry and Burgundy, of the Queen and of the Duchesses. Another very fine staircase, with a double turn, rises in the turret which flanks the west tower, and a ramp leads to the watchtower, both developing around the same spiral.

The grandson of Louis I, René d'Anjou, King of Naples, whose sister, Marie d'Anjou, had married Charles VII, this "good King René", poet, painter and "prince, enamoured of all things which this earth offers man", darling of the Angevins, wanted in turn to embellish the castle which he had taken as a model in his set of allegorical miniatures "le Coeur d'Amour épris". The works, carried out from 1454 to 1472, restored the east tower to a fit state, included the building of a staircase tower in the east corner of the courtyard, and of a square tower on the southeast façade. He also maintained and restored previous buildings.

On his death, the duchy of Anjou returned to the Crown and the castle had a governor and garrison.

In 1589, at the end of the wars of religion, Henry of Navarre, the future Henry IV, obtained Saumur from Henry III, where there were numerous protestants, as a safe place for them. He assigned government of it to Duplessis-Mornay, his ambassador and friend, ordering him to fortify the castle without delay. This was the age of complete systems of defences surrounding the castle: bastions, demilunes, pill-boxes and sentry boxes, forerunners of the fortifications of the century of Louis XIV.

Under the government of Mornay, which lasted 32 years, Saumur became a metropolis of the protestant religion but with complete loyalty to royal power.

Under Louis XIV, the castle became a prison and began to fall into ruin until its purchase, at the beginning of the twentieth century, by the town, which had it restored, and formed there a museum of decorative arts and one concerning horses.

Saumur is in fact a town with a strong equestrian tradition, famous for its riders and riding schools since the sixteenth century.

The Cadre Noir has remained the French academic riding school and now forms part of the National Equestrian School.

Above: Museum of Decorative Arts - the Renaissance room.
Below: earthenware from Nevers and Rouen (Lair collection).
Below right: the Holy Family, polychrome wood (Flanders, sixteenth century).

Museum of Decorative Arts, above: Middle Ages room, "The Dance of the Savages" tapestry.
Opposite: St. Catherine of Alexandria (fifteenth century, France).
Below: "Cadre Noir" High-Jumper and rider performing a Curvet.
Castle roofs and roof ridges.

Right-hand page: Brissac castle, main façade.
Bottom left: the hunting room; right: the theatre.

BRISSAC. Pierre de Brézé, minister of Charles VII and of Louis XI, had built a castle resembling those of Langeais or Ussé. It was sold in 1502 to René de Cossé, chamberlain of Charles VIII. The castle remained with his direct descendants.

Charles II of Cossé-Brissac, one of the leaders of the ultra-Catholic party of the League, appointed Governor of Paris in January 1594, realised that he had to recognise Henry IV as legitimate King of France and end the civil war. On 22 March 1594, the doors of the capital were opened to him; in spite of the fanatics and foreign garrisons, he avoided bloodshed. Henry IV

raised Brissac to a duchy, gave Charles II the marshal's baton and authorised him to rebuild his castle which had suffered during the civil war. The beneficiary devoted his time there, starting from 1606, to a grandiose project which was to make Brissac an unrivalled monument, reaching seven to eight storeys and developing three wings, after the total elimination of the remains of the old castle. Numerous famous architects, sculptors, painters and decorators were engaged on the site. However the Marshal died in 1621, the works stopped and the castle remained incomplete, as we see it now: the main wing, on the east side, still within the two towers of the old

Above: the great drawing-room.

castle is made of a high pavilion in a style similar to that of Cheverny, slightly more Italian, combining, on five storeys, the five classical orders of the pillars, the bossed stones, the pediments, the cartouches and the niches for the statues. The central pavilion has four levels and ends, half-finished, behind the old southeast tower. The north wing, at right angles, more austere and more seventeenth century, is flanked by a tall square pavilion. At the foot of the castle, on the courtyard side, flows the Aubance in the valley meadows. The admirable interior is that of a high family, having maintained, over four centuries, traditions, savoir-vivre and a taste for the arts.

BOUMOIS, built by the baron of Thory at the end of the fifteenth century and the early sixteenth century, was born, like so many other castles and residences of the Loire valley, from a gradual change from late Gothic art to that of the Renaissance and of the equally gradual progression from a war fortress to a country domain. The towers, with their covered way on machicolations and their top floor set back, are younger sisters of those of Ussé or Langeais, the façade over the courtyard and its staircase tower flanked by a turret, are reminiscent of the arrangement of that of Plessis-lès-Tours and a number of seigneurial estates of the end of the fifteenth century. The castle has retained the seigneurial feature of the dovecot built in the seventeenth century.

In 1760 Aristide Dupetit-Thouars was born at Boumois and later died heroically in 1798, at the battle of Aboukir, commanding the vessel "Le Tonnant" which he refused to surrender.

◄

AUGÉ, like many fortresses in the Loire valley, was founded by Foulques Nerra, at the beginning of the eleventh century, although its fame came from René d'Anjou, cousin and brother-in-law of Charles VII. The man people called "good King René" was the most cultured and versatile Prince, even man, of his time. René personally supervised the construction, which began in 1455, of a simple and attractive castle, well-lit, pleasant to live in and near the forest for hunting. Yolanda of Aragon, his mother, and himself, stayed there often. The nearby hospice houses the relic of the real cross known as the cross of Anjou. When the Duke of Anjou became the Duke of Lorraine, the cross of Anjou also became the cross of Lorraine. ►

MONTGEOFFROY. The marquis of Contades, Marshal of France under Louis XV, built, in 1772, the castle on the site of the one his family had bought in the seventeenth century. The two towers of the fifteenth century, on either side of the courtyard, and the sixteenth-century chapel on the right side, are similar to the ancient estate. The architect Barré led the works in a lively manner: from 1776, the castle was finished, perfectly balanced and simple, admirably valorised in the perspective of a long path between the flowerbeds. Better still, it was furnished and decorated; an inventory shows that the furniture, the work of the finest cabinetmakers, the panelling, tapestries and paintings are in their original places, a rare example of an aristocratic interior on the eve of the Revolution. The respect of the inhabitants for the marquis and for his service records protected him and his castle from the revolutionaries. He died in 1795 and the people of the nearby village prevented anyone from touching the property which remained in the family. ▼

LE LUDE. Replacing a simple wooden fort, the Counts of Anjou built a keep in the tenth century. The present castle is built on the walls of a fortress of the thirteenth century: a square outer wall flanked by six towers, surrounded by wide moats, with a cutwater structure in front, over the Loir. During the Hundred Years' War this castle was besieged several times; in 1370 the English lifted the siege. In 1425 Warwick captured the fortress, which was regained in 1427, not without damage. In 1457 Jean de Daillon, in the service of the dauphin, Louis, bought Le Lude in a sorry state. He was a diplomat appreciated by Louis XI who nicknamed him "skilful Jean", he restored the castle. His son Jacques made his name in Italy and on the Pyrenees defending Fontarabie (1522-1523). From 1520 to 1530 Jacques de Daillon and his wife directed rebuilding of the south façade in the style of the early Renaissance: towers and façades are punctuated by the vertical sections of the high windows and superposed pillars, and the horizontal sections of the bands and mouldings marking the levels. Attracted by the fashion in terracotta medallions launched at the castle of Madrid in the Bois de Boulogne for Francis I, the Daillons used stone medallions which decorate the façade and give it its character. Jacques died in 1533 from the wounds he received at Pavia. His son Jean, Count of le Lude, had the interiors fitted out. François succeeded him, serving Henry IV and Louis XIII whom he received on his land. On his death in 1619 his son Timoléon retired there, perfecting the garden and castle. This period dates the "second Renaissance" inner courtyard. In honour of Henry, last of that name, Louis XIV raised Le Lude to a peerage duchy. This great personality, with much wit, lived at the Court, fulfilling important duties. In 1751, Monsieur Du Velaer, trader of the Compagnie des Indes, bought the castle. His heiress, the Marquess de la Vieuville, begged Barré, who had built Montgeoffroy, to build, overlooking the Loire, the Louis XVI façade, an elegant balance of three pavilions; the middle one, slightly projecting, has an emblazoned pediment, the storeys are decorated with niches or medallions. Barré was responsible for the Renaissance façade over the courtyard, closed off, on the town side, by a Louis XVI portico. The Marquess, supported by the inhabitants of Le Lude, saved the castle from the revolutionaries and bequeathed it, through her daughter, to the de Talhouet family of which the present owner, the Countess de Nicolaÿ descended. Bearing in mind the restoration works of the nineteenth century, Le Lude successfully combines some of the main French styles, of the thirteenth and fourteenth centuries. This is in addition to the discovery of a furnished and decorated residence whose historical and cultural heritage is maintained by the owners.

ANGERS

A Gallo-Roman oppidum still occupied, at the end of the third century of our age, the shale promontory over the Maine. It is certain that other fortified complexes, Celtic and prehistoric, had preceded it since the natural site is perfect for defence. The Gallo-Roman wall, five metres wide at its base and three at the top, was still in existence in the ninth century, after the Visigothic and Breton sieges, among other invaders. The Normans captured Angers and kept the town in their power for six years, until Charles the Bald, grandson of Charlemagne, undertook, with the Duke of Brittany, his ally, to divert the Maine. The Vikings could not live without water under their boats and departed

again. Several expeditions brought them back to Angers. The Counts of Anjou, the first dynasty of Angers, built a keep, an outer wall and a chapel in the tenth and eleventh centuries, on the southwestern edge of the rock. Geoffroy, son of Foulques Nerra, having married in 1128 Matilda, daughter of William, Duke of Normandy and King of England, rebuilt the castle on 5,000 square metres on the site of the court of the seigneurs. Some parts of the walls remain. Henry II Plantagenet, his elder son, married the spirited Eleanor of Aquitaine, rejected by Louis VII, King of France, and became, through the inheritance of his mother, King of England. Angers, where he held his court as often as in London, became the continental capital of the King of leopards, under his reign and that of Richard the Lionheart, his son. In 1203, ending the demands of John Lackland, brother and successor to Richard, Philip Augustus joined Angers to the crown, with Maine, Normandy and Brittany. His daughter-in-law, Blanche de Castille and Louis IX, his grandson, built, on the rock of Angers, one of the most powerful fortresses of the kingdom, in the heart of the estate regained from the Plantagenets, which had to be defended against Henry III of England, son of John Lackland.

Louis IX, aged seventeen, arrived at Angers in 1231. The site opened in 1232. Apparently it was ended by around 1238 - 1240. The outer wall built in shale linked by horizontal anchorages of white limestone, measures 952 metres and forms a pentagon of 25,000 square metres. The northwest side has a sheer drop over the Maine, a simple wall being sufficient as any attack was impossible. The other sides are flanked by seventeen round towers, with embankments at the foot. Like at Carcassonne, another fortress of Saint-Louis, the arches are arranged in staggered rows. Each tower is 18 metres in diameter. The north tower, known as the Mill tower, is the same size as all the others, plus machicolation, covered way and rooves. The other six were rased to the level of the curtain walls in 1585 by order of Henry III, so that, the castle falling into the hands of protestants, would be impossible to regain afterwards. The Mill tower remained to set its wings against the west winds and grind flour for the garrison. An eighteenth tower, known as the Guillon tower, outside of the walls, destroyed in 1832, was used for the provisions of the fortress.

Given as a privilege in 1246 by Saint Louis to his brother, Charles I of Anjou, wholly fascinated by the kingdom of Sicily, Angers

was then handed down to his son Charles II, whose daughter married Charles de Valois, father of Philip VI. The latter reunited Anjou to the crown which he donned in 1328. Thus ended the first French house of Anjou. The second one began when Jean II the Good gave Anjou, raised to a duchy, to his son, Louis, Duke of Anjou. Charles, the elder, became King Charles V. In 1367, Louis, an enthusiast of art and architecture like his three brothers (the King who renovated the Louvre, Jean, Duke of Berry, Philippe, Duke of Burgundy) assigned Macé Delarue, his architect, a large part of the works to improve the castle. He also commissioned the painting and weaving of the tapestry of the Apocalypse, a hanging composed of seven equal pieces forming as a whole 144 metres long and 5.5 metres high, woven from 1377 to 1380/1382 by Nicolas Bataille, in Paris, from sketches by Hennequin de Bruges, according to a set of miniatures. The whole tapestry, bequeathed to the cathedral by King René, was thrown out and almost disappeared in the nineteenth century. Seventy scenes out of one hundred and five have been preserved for us and are on display in the gallery of the museum, designed to exhibit them. Louis I, who died in 1384, always faithful and loyal to the King, unlike Burgundy and Berry, was succeeded by Louis II, who married Yolanda of Aragon in 1402 (Charles VII was to be their son-in-law). The Duke and Duchess lived in the castle which they kept in a state of defence. In this vast enclosed estate, they commissioned building of the new chapel and the royal lodging. This rectangular-plan chapel, with a flat apse, built from 1405 to 1413, is covered with three bays of Angevin vaults whose keystones are wonderfully worked.

The tapestry of the Apocalypse illustrates the mysterious book of St. John the Evangelist represented, like the visionary witness, in a niche at the side of each scene (opposite left). The master tapestry-weaver from Paris, Nicolas Bataille, worked from sketches by Jean Bandol, known as Hennequin des Bruges, in the years 1377-1380 or

82. Seven hangings of 12 to 16 pictures, with alternating red and blue backgrounds, covered 144 m by 5.50 m of which 107.50 m remain. Here, from top to bottom, scenes: 29 (chapter XI: 1 - 2), 26 (chapter IX: 16 - 21) and 36 (chapter XII: 7 - 12).

Of the royal loggia only the wing remains which extends the chapel, and a wing at right angles once looked out over the Maine. Their son, King René, continued the works, and had built, in the corner of the west gable of the chapel, the spiral staircase leading to the storeys of the lodging; it is covered by a palm vault, with sixteen segments, separated by prismatic ribbing, keystones and cul-de-lampes with plant motifs, sculpted by masters of the genre. This octagonal-plan staircase on the north gallery led to the loggia which has disappeared, providing access to each room of the storey and to watch the entertainments given in the courtyard of the seigneurs without being dazzled by the sun. King René also built the entrance fort in this formerly closed courtyard; he had designed it and described in 1451 its building in detail. He turned too to the gardens. From his earldom in Provence he sent for flowers and bushes and all kinds of animals from the Barbary coast for his menageries. An inventory of the time allows us to imagine the importance of these lodgings: they numbered fifty-four inhabitable bedrooms, of which only two large ones remain. In 1475 René had to abandon Anjou to his nephew Louis XI and retire to Provence. Louis had the dry moats dug wich, later, Jean de l'Espine widened at the end of the sixteenth century. Jean Bourré, captain of the castle, renewed its artillery. It is only in the year 1562 that the castle was properly adapted to the new techniques of attack and defence of fortresses. Philibert Delorme was assigned to it and entrusted his Angevin friend, Jean de l'Espine, with direction of the works.

Angers was to become, during the following centuries, a citadel and garrison, as well as a prison: Fouquet was a prisoner there. The two Medieval gates are still there: the town gate in the north east and the gate to the fields in the south. Between these two gates is the bailey, a true military esplanade, today a French garden, and the Governor's residence, built in the eighteenth century, preserving a staircase tower of the fifteenth century.

LE-PLESSIS-BOURRÉ

Jean Bourré, close collaborator of Louis XI, during his début as young dauphin, in difficulty with Charles VII, until his death, taking responsibility for everything, including supervision of the upbringing of young Charles, future Charles VIII, had a great stroke of luck which never failed him. He continued to perform his functions as treasurer under the reigns of Charles VIII and Louis XII. From 1465 to 1467 he had Langeais built of which he was captain. On 26 November 1462 he had bought the seigneury of Plessis-le-Vent, in his native Anjou. He was also seigneur of Miré, where he built the castle of Vaux, Jarzé and others. The castle of Plessis, which he built without stopping, starting in 1464, was finished in 1472 (14 January of this year is the date of the transaction for the glass panes of the lodging). Designed to keep the enemy at bay and to remain, therefore, out of reach of its guns, it is a vast rectangle, flanked by four corner towers, fully surrounded by false breeches, platform at the level of the moats for placing and removing the artillery. The high walls built to resist direct attacks by ladders or mobile towers, are no longer justified, only the wing of the seigneurial lodgings has two storeys under the covered way, the three others have only one. A single tower, that of the southeast corner, which was used as a keep, has machicolations. On the curtain walls, they are replaced by vertical grooves formed in the wall to channel the bullets onto any attackers. A 43-metre bridge leads to the double drawbridge fort and

covered way on machicolation, flanked by two turrets. The lodging wing is opposite the entrance, flanked by two staircase turrets. Surrounded by low buildings on three sides, the courtyard is shallow, and from the storeys it is possible to see over the blue slate rooves the Angevin countryside. The wife of Jean Bourré, Marguerite de Feschal, according to some authors is said to have actively contributed to the decision regarding the fittings and decoration of Plessis, as did the wives of other great financiers of the kingdom later at Chenonceau, Azay, and Cheverny. The interiors, chapel, rooms and furnished halls, of great quality, reserve for the visitor the surprise of the guard room whose painted wooden ceiling is decorated with twenty-four paintings illustrating fables, proverbs and allegories, at times insolent, and such that they were described in a chapter of Rabelais. Lovers of exoterism find something to think about and discuss alchemy.

The guard room.

Le Plessis-Bourré: the library.

The large drawing-room.

The main vestibule.

The royal bedroom.

SERRANT

The last but not least of the great castles of the Loire ends our journey along the river.

Its building was begun in the Renaissance age, towards the middle of the century, at the beginning of the reign of Henry II. The seigneury of Serrant belonged to the de Brie family. Ponthus de Brie had obtained from Louis XI around 1421 permission to fortify his castle. The moats are the sole reminder of this castle together with the traditional plan which they indicate, mostly re-used by the new castle. Charles de Brie turned to the greatest name of the time, Philibert Delorme, the architect of Diane de Poitiers and of her royal lover, Henry II. His plans were taken as the basis for the works; unfortunately it appears that Charles de Brie was ruined through them. On his death in 1593 only half of the central block and of the left wing were completed, forming the north corner of the castle.

The property was purchased in 1596 by Hercule de Rohan, Duke of Montbazon, who did nothing with it, apparently, and sold it to Guillaume Bautru, diplomat and academician, of the first generation of the famous assembly of the Académie Française. The ambassador, a literary man, renowned for his wit and remarks, ended the main building. His son, Guillaume, who lived until 1711, finished the wings and replaced by square pavilions the round towers of the fifteenth century, which marked the corners of the courtyard, towards the entrance. He also had the portal built, in line with the castle.

The whole complex whose circumstances extended its building over two centuries, nevertheless is agreeably coherent. The interior of the courtyard is fully built with white tufa and every attempt has been made to adopt a single style, in harmony with the beginning of the fulfilment of the project of Philibert Delorme. The two projecting pavilions contrast with the brown shale of the walls and the anchorages and frames in white tufa, like the three outer façades, which gives them a certain air of austerity. The arrangement of the façades, the superposed pillars (ionic order at the ground floor, corinthian at the storeys) frame the openings onto the courtyard or divided at regular intervals, on the exterior façades, remain in the typical style of the castles of the Loire valley of the late Renaissance, in the same way as the central staircase, with a double straight flight, covered by a coffered vault. Marguerite Bautru, daughter of the second Guillaume, had married the Marquis of Vaubrun, general lieutenant of the King's armies. He died by the side of Turennes, mortally wounded, at the battle of Altenheim in 1675. The Marquess had sculpted by Antoine Coysevox a mausoleum of white marble and built, in the extension of the right wing, a chapel for this mausoleum, by the equally famous Hardouin-Mansart. The Vaubrun daughter, Duchess d'Estrées, sold Serrant in 1749 to Antoine Walsh, officer of the Irish navy, on the side of the Stuarts, whom he had followed in their exile in France. He obtained the title of Count of Serrant. His son and daughter-in-law were introduced into the court of Napoleon and Madame de Serrant was lady-in-waiting to the empress Josephine. Under the Restoration the castle fell, by alliance, to the de la Trémoïlle family, omnipresent in the history of France in the Loire valley. The visit to the interior of the castle, magnificently furnished, reveals the heritage handed down by the generations of a very old family.

INDEX

Photographs Editions Valoire
with the collaboration of P. Viard and R. Nicko,
and the contribution of J.M. Berneron, page 46 (c), Claude Villette, Valérie
Thévenot, pp. 40 and 41; Michel Velut p. 97, p. 136 (b); of © Conseil
Général du Loiret, Photo by Dominique Chauveau, p. 12 (a-b); of
Photélico Berger, p. 14 (b); p. 83 (a); of Héliflash, p. 19 (b), p. 59 (a).
All rights reserved - Reproduction prohibited.
Printed in the EEC - Legal deposit: 2nd quarter 2001
I.S.B.N. 2-909575-37-3